Cultivate Your Relationships the Vastu Way

Cultivate Your Relationships the Vastu Way

DR PREM KUMAR SHARMA

PRABHAT
PAPERBACKS

Published by
PRABHAT PAPERBACKS
An imprint of Prabhat Prakashan Pvt. Ltd.
4/19 Asaf Ali Road,
New Delhi-110002 (INDIA)
e-mail: prabhatbooks@gmail.com

ISBN 978-93-5488-402-3

CULTIVATE YOUR RELATIONSHIPS THE VASTU WAY!
by Dr Prem Kumar Sharma

Edition
First, 2023

Price
₹ 350 (Rupees Three Hundred Fifty Only)

Printed at
Japan Art, Delhi

I dedicate this book, with deepest regards and affection, to
my parents whose inspiration
has taught me to share and care.

I bow to Maa Goddess Kali whose benevolence
and blessings has bestowed me with
divine powers and the wisdom to use
them in the service of others.

Records

ASIA Book of Records

Dr Prem Kumar Sharma is titled as "Grand Master" for writing a unique book on Vaastu to cater to all relationships.

"Cultivate Your Relationships the Vaastu Way" has made a record and entered into Asia Book of Records in the year 2020.

India Book of Records

"Cultivate Your Relationships the Vaastu Way" has made it to India Book of Records in the year 2020.

Author's Note

Relationships and Vastu? Never heard of it? This is probably the first book that exclusively deals with Vastu's influence on relationships. The present-day Vastu experts continue to deal with the effects of inanimate objects on the occupants of a house or workplace but fail to explore their influence on relationships between the members occupying the house in any detail.

We, being social animals, interact with one another at all times throughout our lives. From birth to death, our success or failure is measured by the kind of relationship we have had with others. We nurture friendships, indulge in romances, consolidate work and school-related connections, strengthen family ties, and quite often, get involved in relationships that defy categorization! Relationships are central to our existence, yet none is simple or can be taken for granted. If cultivated properly, they have the potential to enrich us, adding to our feelings of self-worth, enjoyment and growth. On the other hand, there are relationships that may make us uncomfortable. Family not treating us properly, spouse cheating on us, children getting out of hand, lovers being dishonest, colleagues back-stabbing, elders not getting the respect they deserve and the like. Remember that in all kinds of kinships, there is bound to be some disagreement, need for compromise and times of frustration, but they don't necessarily make a relationship unhealthy.

Through my years devoted to solving people's problems through Astrology, I have found unhappiness afflicting a majority of households, mostly resulting from strained inter-personal relationships between family members. This friction, occurring between mothers and daughters-in-law, amongst brothers, between teenage children and their parents or between others, if left unattended, generally becomes a sure shot recipe for disaster. It would not have been possible for me to carry out this relationship study without the help of the men, women and children who were generous enough to share with me their experiences of family and professional life. I am grateful to them for their frank discussions of situations, which were often very painful for them.

In addition to Astrology, Vastu Shastra, the ancient treatise on architecture, is another powerful science that emphasizes ways to attain happiness by correct citing of the building and placement of the components within. It has a wealth of information on the enhancement of human relationships. I have studied it in detail and am surprised to find that the principles and techniques available in this treatise can be employed to the restoration and cultivation of relationships too. This has afforded me a fresh look at the application of Vastu principles. For example, before I commence with the remedial measures for, say, health problems afflicting a household, my first step is to find out the interpersonal equation within the house. Are the people getting along fine within the house or are there some tensions? Only this approach gives me the full picture of what ails a house.

I have meticulously collected the relevant material of Vastu's influence on relationships after an in-depth study of Vastu Shastra and am happy to present it in the form of this book. So, pick up this book if you want to cultivate your relationships with others. It is presented in an easy-to-use format that touches upon only the practical aspects of Vastu application, sparing you all inessential details. Read it at leisure, implement its easy-to-follow tips and suggestions, and see your relationships blossom!

Jai Mata Di

– Dr Prem Kumar Sharma

Introduction

Why are some homes happy and some full of woe? Why are some buildings more prone to family discords while others most conducive to happy relationships within the family? Is it merely because of the people inhabiting the structure or does the building have an influence of its own? It is evident that happiness is not the privilege of the rich alone who live in big bungalows. Big houses can be as unhappy as small hovels in slums. On the contrary, a hut with just the bare necessities of life can be overflowing with happiness whilst a palace with all the comforts of the world can be full of sorrow.

Almost everyday we hear of the sad incidents of wife-burning, child molestation, ill treatment of the aged and other family discords in the houses of both the rich and the poor. Such homes require great tact and patience to sustain a cordial atmosphere. We may attribute this happiness or sadness to the nature of individual family members. But who shapes their nature? We often find that a person who is jovial and life-of-the-party outside becomes moody and irritable at home. Building healthy relationships needs work patience, tolerance and compassion. However,

Vastu Shastra maintains that it is the structure that influences the occupants of a building and not the other way round. It blames the construction of the building and the arrangements within for this transformation because the same individual, who was cheerful in the company of his own family members outside the house, becomes irritable, once inside!

Vastu Shastra considers happiness to be one of the most important and fundamental constituents of any relationship. According to it, happiness is not just about wealth, fame and prosperity, but about harmony in all relationships, be it within our immediate family—our parents, brothers or sisters, or our children—or amongst close friends, colleagues and acquaintances. Adherence to the principles of Vastu can transform unhappy lives into happier ones by balancing the energies of the cosmic universe to create harmony with nature and each other and make the occupants of a house or workplace happy by improving mutual relationships. Therefore, Vastu Shastra lays great stress on the correct citing of the building and the placement of the components within.

This book is a voyage of discovery that explores relationships in the context of Vastu. It is presented in an easy to grasp question-answer format that attempts to solve actual relationship problems by Vastu techniques. Broadly organised into three main parts for easy reference, it deals with relationships within and outside the family, and at the workplace.

All Vastu methods for happy relationships and family luck are contained in this book. By designing our place of work and residence according to the principles of Vastu, we can enhance positive energies and diminish negative ones, achieving not only prosperity but also stable relationships within the household.

Having said this, it is pertinent to mention that the domain of relationships is one of the most difficult areas of human life. The closer the ties, the harder are the challenges. Relationship with people nearest to us, such as spouses, parents, children, siblings, or close friends and relatives, can become a source of our deepest anxieties, fears, insecurities, unhappiness or pain. Most relationship problems can be overcome through Vastu techniques presented in this book, but in certain cases where the problem persists, it will be most prudent to approach a Vastu expert, who is trained to suggest appropriate remedial measures by detailed study of the house in the context of the problem.

The world of relationships is waiting to be explored the Vastu way. So, just delve into this book, follow the given tips and suggestions and find your cup of happiness overflow!

❑

Vastu–An Overview

Vastu Shastra, a voluminous treatise containing a diverse collection of independent works on architecture, iconography and art, was thought to have developed between 6000 BC and 3000 BC according to modern historians Ferguson, Havell and Cunningham. Its use was restricted only to the architects of those times and was passed down to successive generations by word of mouth or through hand-written monographs.

The word 'Vastu' is derived from a Sanskrit word *vaas* meaning 'to dwell' and 'Shastra' meaning 'a treatise'. This traditional Indian system of architecture and design of Vedic origin considers Earth as the principal Vastu and takes into its fold the site where the building is to be constructed, the structure of the building and the placement of the components within.

The first direct reference to Vastu Shastra is found in Stapatya Veda, a constituent of Atharva Veda. Some important works on Vastu are Manasara, Mayamata, Brihat Samhita, Viswakarma Prakasha and Samarangana Sutradhara. It also finds mention in the *Ramayana* and the *Mahabharata*. It is believed that town planning of the ancient city of Ayodhya shows many parallels to a city described in ancient Manasara. The first official treatise on Vastu, the Kasyapa Silpa, has been attributed to Sage Kasyapa. Agama Shastra, on the science of temples, considers Vastu as the basis for any type of construction. Excavations at Harappa and Mohenjodaro also indicate the influence of Vastu on the Indus Valley Civilization.

Vastu Shastra aims at bringing people in harmony with nature by balancing the energies of the cosmic universe. Ancient town planners and house builders laid great emphasis on bestowing harmony to the site or building for the peace and prosperity of the occupant. If Vastu principles are followed religiously, they ensure happiness, health, peace and tranquility. According to Vastu Shastra, our place of work and residence should be so designed that positive energies dominate the negative ones for all round happiness and prosperity of the occupants.

The Vastu Purush

Vastu Purush, said to be the spirit of the site, is an important deity in Vastu Shastra. If he is not appeased before the commencement of construction, nothing but misfortune will result. Only when he is placated with the spirit bless and protect the construction. There are many interesting mythological stories concerning the origin of Vastu

Purush. One version is mentioned in the Matsya Purana. Once Shiva, engaged in a fierce battle with a rakshasa or demon called Andhikasur, began to tire and started sweating profusely. As the beads of perspiration fell, a demon was created out of them. This demon was so massive that he obstructed the Earth and the sky with his huge body. This alarmed the devtas or Gods, who seized him and sat on his back, sending him hurtling down towards the Earth. The demon, under the immense weight of as many as 45 Gods, crashed to the Earth. He lay prone, face down with his head towards the north-east and feet towards the south-west, pinned by all the Gods sitting on his back.

In order to save his life, he prayed to Brahma, "Oh Lord, you have created this cosmos. This body is also yours. Why then are these Gods torturing me without reason? Tell me how should I behave with the Gods?" Brahma, moved by the sincerity of his prayers, said, "Since this moment, your worship shall be indispensable in every auspicious construction work because of your presence beneath the Gods. After building any structure, people who offer you prayers and worship you as Vastu devta will be blessed with happiness and prosperity. Those who do not worship you for any reason shall have to suffer penury and untimely death. They shall have to face your wrath and encounter obstacles in everything they do." From that day onwards, Vastu Purush was born and the Gods, sitting on the various locations on his back, became the presiding deities of their respective directions.

Whether this story is true or just an interesting folklore is difficult to say. However, one thing is certain that Vastu Shastra is no myth and has stood the test of time for thousands of years.

The Science of Directions

Simply stated, Vastu Shastra is the science of directions. It aims at harnessing the energies of different directions for our prosperity. It specifies directions for everything from eating to sleeping and from working to decorating the house. The directions, governed by the respective ruling deities, dictate the most ideal locations for rooms and arrangements within. If any element is not located or placed in proper direction, it causes defect and compromises the auspiciousness of the place. Removing the defect entails rectification of architecture.

There are a total of eight directions – the four cardinal points: north, south, east and west; and its four conjunctions: north-east, south-east, north-west and south-west.

North: The north is governed by Kuber, the God of Wealth and Soma, the Lord of Health. This direction is associated with tranquility, relaxation and sexual relationships. If a master bedroom is made in this direction one can expect a stable sex life and a peaceful, contented marital relationship. This is also a good zone for spiritual studies or meditation and for receiving inner guidance and developing extrasensory awareness. This sector also enhances the healing properties of medicines. It should not be blocked, as it is the source of female issues. Its element is water and its colour is black.

North-east: Eesh, the lord of energy and knowledge, governs the north-east. This direction is associated with self-awareness and knowledge. It energizes those who need to be clear about their direction in life and provides emotional drive and motivation to them for achieving the same. This strong motivational energy also makes it a good sector for sports and physical activities. But being the God's abode, this direction should always be kept vacant. Its element is earth and its colour is blue.

East: East is governed by Indra, the king of Gods. It is the predominant direction because the sun, the giver of life, rises from this direction bringing with it its divine influence. The energy from the east provides contentment, optimism and encouragement to look towards the future in a more positive frame of mind. It infuses the dispirited and depressed with positive energy, enabling them to enjoy good health. This direction also favours family generations and ensures long life for the owner of the house. It should never be blocked and some open space should always be provided in this direction, since it is the source of male issues. Its element is wood and its colour is green.

South-east: Agni, the God of Fire, governs the south-east. This direction is associated with heat. It influences health, wealth and prosperity in all its forms and promotes creativity and natural abilities to help individuals find new ways of solving stubborn problems. If this sector is defective then the inmates of the house become ill tempered. Being associated with heat and creativity, this corner is particularly good for preparing food. Its element is wood and its colour is purple.

South: The south is governed by Yama, the God of Death. This direction is most favourable for wealth, success, happiness and peace. People who are in business, and need to entertain both potential and existing clients and business associates, must take advantage of its strong energy. The energy of the south is also favourable for passion and can help re-ignite the spark of carnal pleasures. Its element is fire and colour is red.

South-west: Niriti, the Lord of Demons and Goddess of Destruction, governs the south-west. The energy of this direction bestows tranquility and purity. It is particularly helpful in building and maintaining strong relationships that help generate a firm underlying trust amongst the family members. It also bestows a humble nature and good character to the residents, encouraging practicality to help solve all kinds of problems. It provides character and longevity. Its element is earth and its colour is pink.

West: The west is governed by Varuna, the God of Water and Rain, and Upholder of the Universal Law. The energy of this direction is associated with success glory, fame and fortune. This energy also promotes love amongst family members and their overall prosperity. It makes children feel loved and safe, and helps them overcome emotional childhood difficulties. Its element is metal and its colour is white.

North-west: Vaayu, the God of Wind, governs the north-west. The energy of this direction promotes sense of responsibility and ability to plan, organise and lead. This direction affects both business and social life and can help one to optimise the energies for accomplishing any task. It benefits employees seeking promotion and persons wanting to enhance their social life. This direction also influences friendship and enmity. If this sector is defective then one makes a lot of enemies, but if this sector is flawless, one will have many helpful friends. Its element is metal and its colour is grey.

Centre: The centre, ruled by Brahma, the Creator of the Universe, does not belong to any of the directions. This central zone has the most powerful energy and is associated with good physical, spiritual and emotional health. The eight directional energies also influence this area. It is best to leave this zone absolutely clutter-free or the inhabitants may not enjoy good health. Its element is earth and its colour is yellow.

Vastu Basics

Grasping the essentials of Vastu is important for the understanding of this science. Once understood, it can be applied safely in every situation without making any serious mistakes. Make a note of the following basics of Vastu and use them to your advantage.

(a) Square and rectangle shaped plots are the most ideal.

(b) Plots with all the four corners at right angles are the best.

(c) Plot with a longer north-south than east-west axis is most preferable

(d) Plot should not be cut at any corner.

(e) North or east-facing plots are most auspicious.

(f) Plots with corners exactly aligned to the cardinal directions are inauspicious.

(g) Plot should be sloping from the south-west to the north-east.

(h) Extension of plot in any direction other than north-east is not considered favourable.

(i) No road should terminate at a plot or a house.

(j) A plot with roads on all four sides is the most auspicious.

(k) The south west should be the highest point of a house and the north-east the lowest.

(l) The south-west of a house should be the heaviest and the north-east the lightest.

(m) A compound wall should always enclose a building.

(n) The slant of the roof should be from the south-west to the north-east.

(o) Overhead water tanks are best located in south-west and underground tanks in north-east.

(p) Main entrance to the house should be obstruction free.

(q) Drains of the house should flow towards the north-east.

(r) North-east, the sacred corner of the house is ideal for a prayer room.

(s) The master bedroom of the house should always be in the south-west.

(t) Never sleep with head facing towards the north.

(u) Never sleep or sit under a beam.

(v) Kitchen should be in the south-east.

(w) The centre of the house should not be cluttered and should be left vacant.

(x) The best location for a staircase is in the south or south-west of the house.

(y) The width of an ideal door should be half its height.

(z) Windows should be even in number, but the number should not contain a zero.

Once the construction on the plot is completed or a house or flat acquired, thank Vastu Purush and offer him a prayer for harmony and peace:

"Oh Lord, you are the owner of this site. We have come here to live. Please know us. Treat us as your family members. Remove all our problems and help us in maintaining cordial relations among ourselves. Bless us free from all troubles and sorrows. Accept our offerings and please leave this site so that we can occupy the same and live happily in peace

❑

Contents

Part I

Relationships Within the Family

PART ONE

Relationships Within the Family

> *"All happy families resemble one another. Each unhappy family is unhappy in its own way"*
>
> **– Leo Tolstoy, *War and Peace***

The joint family concept in our country has remained largely intact despite an increasing preference of most urbanites to adopt the Western model of the family. Though, on the face of it, it seems that more and more city-dwelling folks are reluctant to keep their elders with them yet in reality, they are still in a minority. For the majority, it is a tradition that is unquestioningly followed generation after generation and can be found in most urban and almost all rural families. This arrangement remains most pragmatic even today where elders are cared for by their children and they in turn instill stability to the household. However, as education makes inroads and individuals begin to think for themselves, the set roles in a joint family have started to be questioned. This, at times, results in relationships being strained to their limits.

Today, a joint family witnesses a lot of power play amongst its members. There is the father who does not want to let go of his authority in the house, especially if the house belongs to him. There is the mother who resents giving up running of the house to her daughter in-law and despises the way she performs her daily chores. There is the son who lays claim to being the head of the house, simply on the basis of being the sole breadwinner. Then there is the daughter-in-law who wants to run her writ in the house and wants to change everything to her way of thinking. And, if by chance, there are other relations sharing the house, they too demand their place in the sun, contributing to the complexity of mutual existence!

In our culture, where arranged marriages are a norm rather than an exception, we have to contend with another problem—that of relationship between couples. It is a fact that each individual is different in nature and has to compromise and adjust to the nature of his or her spouse for a happy family life. But if the couple is a complete ideological mismatch, problems ensue almost immediately. The husband may be short tempered or uncouth, having little respect for his wife. He may be a drunkard, a wife beater or unfaithful. He, being a typical mama's boy, may succumb to the manipulations of his mother against his wife. The wife may be from a totally different background and may feel trapped in a house that does not respect her and treats her like a servant. She may resent her husband's uncaring attitude towards her and their children. She may take a dislike for her in-laws and may be unwilling to look after them.

Then there are the children to contend with, within a family. They have their own wishes and desires. If the parents are uncaring or too involved with themselves, there is every likelihood of their falling into bad company. If not brought up in the right manner, they may harbour resentment against one or both the parents.

It has been observed that in most joint families, in addition to the aged parents, sons and daughters-in-law have to care for other elders too, who have no children of their own to fall back upon. This puts added strain on the household, since they cannot just be wished away.

Maintaining loving relationships within a joint family is a challenge whether in the West or in our country. However, quite evidently, money plays an important role in improving or marring these relationships. If the family is financially secure, most problems sort themselves out, but if there is monetary hardship, more often than not, it leads to petty squabbles within the family that can go to any extreme like dowry deaths, property feuds, etc.

How do we ensure that our family remains happy together? Ancient Vastu scholars had laid great emphasis on the happiness of the household through correct layout and construction of the house and the arrangements within. According to them, adherence to the principles of Vastu can not only accord harmony to the occupants but also confer good health and prosperity. Let us take a look at the various relationships within the house and what Vastu Shastra recommends for improving them.

❑

Chapter 1

Relationship with In-Laws

Lata was married in a grand wedding ceremony to Dhruv, a senior executive with a multinational firm. And from that day on, she had turned from Lata, the individual, to someone's wife and entered a new home with unknown faces claiming to be her new relatives. Though her facial expressions reflected her happiness, internally she was apprehensive as she conjured up the images of overbearing in-laws shown on television serials and movies. She wanted to return to her old life and her freedom which she had left behind. But the truth was that she was married, for better or for worse, and had reached a point of no return. There was a new life to be led and a new role to be played.

From the moment Lata entered her adopted house, it did not take long for this newness to pale and for the power equations to be reworked within the family. Her husband, though passionately in love with her, was totally in control of his mother. Her dictatorial mother in-law seemed a fearful blend of school matron, food inspector, home supervisor, chief chef and hygiene inspector, all rolled into one. Then there was the retired father-in-law who found in her someone to order around once again. Adding to her problems was the unmarried sister-in-law, who had suddenly rediscovered her brother and took upon herself to advise Lata on his likes and dislikes.

Welcome to the joint family. If you have been born and brought up in India, the above scenario would have surely sounded mild against your own individual experiences! This quite familiar setting is a reality in every joint family set-up. A few decades ago, most newly-weds acquired in-laws who were known to them and their parents long before their wedding day. Today, most married couples typically know little about their spouse's family till it is too late.

I have come across plenty of young brides who are just not prepared to adjust to the new environment of a joint family and are always striving to move away along with their husbands. I have also met many husbands who have been reduced to quivering heaps in the fight between their wives and mothers and, in turn, can't stand the sight of their own mothers-in-law.

If you are already or are about to become the victim of a joint family then Vastu Shastra can come to your aid. I have reproduced certain live situations with suggested Vastu remedies, aimed at resolving your relationship problems to a large extent.

Mother-in-law Woes

> Ours have been an inter-caste marriage after a short love affair. Since then we have

been staying with my husband's parents. Though I want to move out, my husband doesn't want to leave them. My problem is my domineering mother in-law who is always trying to create a rift between us. I continue to have fights with my husband on this account. Is there a Vastu cure to overcome this problem?

Since the time marriage was recognized as an institution, the relationship between a mother-in-law and her daughter-in-law has remained turbulent, especially in India. Here a man marries a woman, but woman marries the whole family. Though, on the face of it, a mother-in-law gets a new daughter and the daughter-in-law a new mother yet the latter soon realises that she is meant to pander to the whims and fancies of the entire household. She has to adjust not only to her husband but also to his mother whose notoriety continues to be depicted in movies and television soaps.

To establish themselves in the household, some daughters are tutored to declare war against the newly acquired relatives from day one. Some are advised to cater only to their spouses, ignoring the in-laws. However, much of these antics depend upon the nature of individuals, but the most successful are those who make their adopted home their own. The sooner you do that the happier you would be. Isolating yourself from your in-laws will gain you nothing but frustration, whereas tolerating their idiosyncrasies and adapting yourself to them will increase your chances for a happy family life. As a first step in solving your problems with your mother-in-law, you must find out why she picks on you. It may be that she is right in her judgement of things and you overreact and interpret her ordinary remarks as taunts.

Vastu Tips

Whatever be the issues between you and your mother in-law, Vastu can rid you of these day-to-day tensions. To enhance the relationships with your in-laws, it requires a really strong south-west corner in your home. It is particularly helpful in building and maintaining strong relationships that help generate a firm underlying mutual trust among the family members. It also bestows a humble nature and good character to the occupants, encouraging practicality to help solve all kinds of problems. This sector also affects the mother of the family as well as the household's general well-being regarding domestic life. So, the master bedroom of your in-laws should be in the south-west. If your in-laws are sleeping in some other room, persuade them to shift into this one. And please use tact while you suggest this change! The best person to tackle this job is your husband, of course!

If you are newly-weds, it is advisable that you occupy the bedroom towards the north-west. This, being the quadrant of air, stimulates desire and helps to keep your husband on your side, limiting his mother's influence on him. Ensure that this sector is flawless. If it is defective, for example, if one of the corners is cut, then you will remain at loggerheads with your in-laws, but if this sector is flawless, you will be able to cultivate cordial relations at home. So, make these changes at home and become the real daughter of your mother-in law!

Husband Hates In-laws

> I have a loving husband who dotes on me and gives me every comfort possible. However, I still have a problem. The mere mention of visiting my parent's place spoils his mood for no apparent reasons, despite the respect and care he gets from them. Things have gone so bad that now he would find excuses to avoid going to my place. How can Vastu help me in making my husband love my parents?

A husband's relationship with his in-laws has always been a touchy subject. You must remember that in India, a husband marries only the girl and not her family! It is here that a son-in-law is always an over pampered guest whose tantrums are tolerated smilingly by his in-laws, not wanting to offend him. Despite this, a love-hate relationship continues between the two.

There may be many reasons for your husband not liking your parents. It may be that your father is ideologically very different from your husband. He may be an intellectual and your husband may not be or vice versa. Your mother may be very demanding and expecting your husband to run around her. Or she may be sickly sweet to him, making him bolt. Whatever may be the case, it is up to you to identify what exactly is vexing your husband about your parents. The best way is to listen patiently and without interruptions whenever your husband complains about your parents. Most women find it difficult to tolerate anything negative about their parents and, therefore, fail to notice why their husbands harbour such resentments. Without knowing the reason, you will never be able to find the solution.

A better way is to approach your husband directly and ask him why he behaves the way he does with your parents. In most cases, he will let loose his list of grouses. Listen to him with understanding, if you really want to make him love your parents.

Once you have noted your husband's pet grouses, you should tactfully present them to your parents. Remember that they are old and may not understand what is ailing their son-in-law. Once you have made them aware of what irritates your husband about them, they will, in most cases, curb themselves. On your part, you should also avoid creating situations where your husband has to spend extended time with your parents, since his frustration will only increase. This is not to say that your husband has nothing to do with your parents, but it is just to keep him at a safe distance till love blossoms between the two all by itself.

Vastu Tips

Vastu Shastra has many techniques to restore the bonhomie between your husband and your parents. According to it, if the house suffers from major afflictions such as missing corners, disproportionate weights, faulty slopes, etc., it generates negative energies that show up as ill will between parents and children. So, inspect your parent's house. If it is elevated on the north-east and depressed on the south-west then it is negatively affecting the occupants leading to misunderstandings. Take steps to restore the Vastu basics of an elevated south-west and depressed north-east by adding a room or a shed on the roof towards the south west. This will give you immediate results and you will find cordial relations being restored between your husband and your parents, whenever he visits your parents' place.

Keeping real white flowers in the north corner at the parent's house would help in removing the misunderstandings with son-in-law or the near ones. Also putting Swastika sign on the wooden door on the entrance of the house would help in raising the positive energies in the house and maintaining peace and prosperity.

Grouchy Father-in-law

> We are a middle class family living in an apartment. In addition to my husband and our two little children, my father-in-law is also staying with us. He is a widower and over the years, especially after the death of my mother in-law, has grown quite grumpy. He finds fault with everything and has even started interfering in my household chores. This irritates me no end and my complaints to my husband generally fall on deaf ears. This habit of my father-in-law is causing tension in the family since we can neither leave him to fend for him nor get close to him because of his obnoxious nature. Is there a Vastu way out of this dilemma?

As people grow old, they begin to move towards senility. Their faculties weaken and they retract into a world of their own. Since all other members of the house are busy and have little time for elders, loneliness becomes a severe affliction with them, especially if their spouse, with whom they had shared their life, is no more beside them. In order to get over this boredom and to show that they are still capable of contributing positively to the house, they start to meddle in household work. This unwelcome intrusion becomes the bone of contention between him and the lady of the house and problems ensue.

Since you are facing such a situation, it is best that you don't confront the old man, since he may not understand and take an affront to it. If he is an introvert type, take the initiative to introduce him to other oldsters of the colony. The best opportunity for you to introduce him to his new friends is the get-together party of colony's residential welfare association. This way he will have someone to share his time and interests. If your father-in-law had pursued a hobby before, reintroduce it to him. He will love to start all over again.

Vastu Tips

In case he is not enthusiastic about the above steps, Vastu can help curb his nature to a certain extent. Find out the direction of his room. It should never be in the southeast portion of the house. It would be like adding fuel to fire. Southeast corner belongs to *Agni* and will heat up an already hot temperament. His grumpy nature will be curtailed once he is relocated in a room towards the north of the house.

Removing clutter from his room and keeping them at right places would generate new spirits and render good sleep, which is must for every one. Room freshener and white and purple flowers in the west corner would work miraculous.

Girl Child Curse

I belong to a conservative family and got married at the age of 20 after completing my graduation. Although my mother-in-law is quite overbearing, my troubles really began when I gave birth to a daughter. My mother-in-law, who was expecting a boy, refuses to touch her. Is there a Vastu solution to make her love the child?

Girl child is still regarded as the bane of most Indian households. And their greatest enemies are women themselves. What you are experiencing in your house is not a unique case. There are thousands of such homes where a daughter is aborted even before she sees the light of the day. You should feel lucky that your daughter is with you and the only thing remains for you is to soften your mother-in-law's attitude towards her.

It has been observed that most conservative women of the ilk of your mother-in-law have suffered the same fate or worse. It may be possible that she is applying what she has herself undergone as a young bride, just out of force of habit. She may not be holding any ill will against your daughter, but, it is quite possible that her other frustrations are being expressed through this issue. The trick is to find out what is actually bothering her. The desire for a boy may be a front for her real problem. If you are able to put your finger on it and do something about it, you will find your daughter's innocent antics automatically attracting her maternal instincts. And, within no time, your daughter will be happily cooing in the arms of your mother-in-law.

Vastu Tips

However, for this to happen, ensure that your house and the arrangements within are as per the principles of Vastu. Ensure that the bedroom of your in-laws is in the south-west. This will calm your mother-in-law's nature and make her more receptive. Since your daughter is small, it is best for you to occupy a north-east room. This will infuse positive energies in your daughter and enable her to captivate all through her antics. Making a *pooja* on the north-east sacred corner will also enhance love.

Putting Lord Ganesha's picture on the north wall of your house or the drawing room would help in building good relations among the family members along with good prosperity.

Forced to Retire

> I am in a government job, with three years to retirement. My daughter-in-law left work to look after her baby. She now says I should take voluntary retirement so she can return to work. I've had a fulfilling professional life and want the same for her. But taking retirement now would mean sacrificing those benefits those accrue on completing my tenure. Can Vastu help me come out of this predicament?

You want to continue working. That's fair enough. You invested a lifetime in your profession and it would be a pity to let go of the benefits. And you are being sensitive to your daughter-in-law's needs. The solution to the problem is to see who can look after the baby while you are both at work. A brainstorming session may help generate options. Instead of taking sole responsibility for this problem, sit down with the family and share your thoughts. I'm sure they will be able to appreciate your position and arrive at a suitable decision. And if all this doesn't help, know that you have a right to your life. You can't be babysitting your children or for your children all your life and all of theirs!

Vastu Tips

There is a need for you to be strong to stand up to what you think is right for you. Take the suggestions offered by Vastu to enhance positive, strength-giving energies that may even entail making certain structural changes. If your front door aligns directly with a staircase, there is a tendency for the house's positive energies to be lost. Because the staircase circulates the energies with people constantly moving up and down, it creates an energy flow that leaves the house if it is directly aligned with the main door. Depending on what direction the door is and what kind of energies the residents have, there will be different effects on the people living inside. In case such is the case with your house, this is not the best entry to use. In this case, an alternative entry should be used and this front door should be closed or used occasionally for guests. However, if this is the only door for entering the house, put up a screen between the staircase and door. Plants can also be used to make the energies in this area stronger to prevent energy loss. This step will enhance your standing in the house and help you tide over your predicament.

Estranged Son

> Our son has married inter-caste and stays in a different city because of which our relationship with him is limited. His wife, though nice, seems to find it difficult to accept us and has also influenced our son to question our ways. They have a little girl born last summer who is our first grandchild. I long to meet and hold her, but they are extremely possessive and are reluctant to let us see her. Can Vastu help in changing their view?

There is nothing to get alarmed about, since your son is doing the balancing act between you and his wife. Remember, adult children need distance and closeness, often at the same time, which can be frustrating for parents. Your feeling of loss is understandable, since letting go of a child that you have nurtured and cared for many years can be quite difficult, even after they are adults. Accept that this is a normal feeling. Also remember, you don't have to be a perfect parent. Just as you have to accept the imperfections in your child, he will also learn to accept your imperfections.

As regards your first grandchild, remember that it is also their first child, so some protectiveness as you have noticed is not unusual. Do visit the baby by all means, but be sensitive towards letting your son and his wife decide when it is appropriate for you to share the baby and asking their opinions on gifts. Your mere presence with them will help them change their views.

Vastu Tips

According to Vastu Shastra, human behaviour is influenced by the structure of the building. It is possible that the house in which your son and daughter-in-law stay is not meeting the requirements of Vastu. On your next visit, see if the approach to their bedroom is through a narrow corridor. This experience to some people can be scary due to which they may suffer from clinical claustrophobia. Moreover, the bedroom at the end of a narrow corridor may be the recipient of a build-up of negative energies. There may not be a structural remedy, but you can 'widen' the passage figuratively by placing a mirror on the wall. Psychologically, anyone passing down this corridor will drop negative thoughts the minute he sees his face in the mirror! This will surely influence your children to get out of negativity and change their thinking about you.

❑

Chapter 2

Relationship between Husband and Wife

Aarti heard a familiar knock on the door and immediately knew that Anil was back from the office. Her little daughter Sandhya, who was playing nearby, shouted with joy, "Daddy is home." Aarti hurriedly picked up Sandhya and rushed to the door to give a warm welcome to her husband. Anil greeted them happily and, taking Sandhya in his arms, sank into his favourite chair. Aarti started preparing tea as she briefed him on the day's happenings. Over tea, the couple continued their cheerful banter, interrupted by Sandhya, time and again, who wanted her daddy all to herself.

As the evening wore on, Aarti realised that Anil was getting a bit annoyed for no apparent reason even though he had returned from the office quite cheerful. Very soon his pleasant conversation turned to nitpicking and comments to cutting remarks. Though his mood swing had caught her unawares, she continued to endure him. But when he started taunting her for not doing enough for Sandhya, she could bear it no more. And, before they realised it, they were at each other's throat. Later, Aarti realised that this had been happening for the past several days and felt guilty, thinking she was to blame.

What had caused this unexpected reaction? Was it something that was bothering Anil in the office or was she in the wrong? It could not have been the office because he had returned quite cheerful and did not complain about anything or anyone. They had been married for six years now and had been quite committed to each other before they shifted into this new flat. Anil was a successful businessman, a loving husband and a responsible father. His mood swings were a cause for alarm and Aarti didn't know what to do.

Very often we come across this kind of a situation in our homes, where a happy couple does hurtful things that he or she had never done before, seemingly without reason. Vastu Shastra puts the blame for this unhappiness squarely on the house and the arrangements within. According to it, an incorrectly built or laid out house has a telling influence on relationships that can upset the harmony within. To bring joy back into the house, one has to first find out what faults lie within and then employ methods for its rectification.

I have collected a number of situations in which a couple may find itself and have suggested Vastu remedies for each one of them. These have been derived from the various queries that I continue to receive everyday. Since it is not possible to include all the situations in this book, I have selected those that cover major aspects of spousal relationships. Try the Vastu remedies given herein and you will be surprised to find your relationship perking up with your husband.

Unhelpful Husband

> My husband never helps in the household chores, though we are both working. I have to get up at six every morning to prepare meals for all, dress up the children and accompany them to school, where I also teach. But my husband, who starts late for his office, doesn't bother to tidy up the house after I am gone and leaves it for me to do on my return. When I broach this subject to him, he gets irked. Though he is loving and caring, I feel that he takes me too much for granted. Is there a remedy for this in Vastu Shastra?

Yours is not a unique problem. Most Indian husbands think that housework is only for their wives and they themselves are meant exclusively for earning. This division of labour is fine when the wife is not working and staying at home, but in the present time where both couples are earners, the equation changes drastically. Still, in most Indian homes, working wives continue to be burdened with all their housewifely duties in addition to holding a proper job.

In order to overcome this inequality in sharing of housework, your first step should be to explain your feelings about the issue to your husband. Do it tactfully and not in a complaining manner or your husband may get irritated. If your husband is loving and caring, as you have mentioned, he would certainly be open to suggestions. Since husbands generally want to help around the house, they need to be told in detail how to go about it. Teach him specifically, what all you want of him and how. However, if he is still unwilling to share the burden despite your insistence, then there is a problem. It can be directly attributed to his lack of concern for you and you may need to do something about it.

Vastu Tips

Vastu Shastra suggests techniques to enhance love. The first step is to find out the direction of your bedroom. A bedroom in the south-west is particularly helpful in building and maintaining strong relationships between couples. It helps generate love and understanding in both spouses. This direction also gives wisdom to solve all kinds of problems. So, make your master bedroom in the south-west direction of your house. If you cannot shift to a room in this direction, don't despair. You can rectify your existing room too by arranging it in the Vastu way. Keep the north-east, the sacred corner, free. Place the bed in such a manner that your feet don't point towards this corner. Use a double bed prepared from a single log of wood. This will strengthen the bond between you two. Use a single mattress and not two separate mattresses on this double bed. This will help generate feeling of sharing, making your husband more inclined to help you around the house.

If possible try to get your bed walls painted light pink or light blue. Also keep Red flowers in the south-west or west corner of your bedroom and keep some plants on the entrance of the door of your house to energize your house with positive energies and also to raise the levels of love energy among the family members.

Moody Wife

> Of late I am experiencing a peculiar problem. Whenever I return home from office I always find my wife quite moody and instead of welcoming me, she complains some thing or the other. She always tries to make me feel guilty for not doing enough for her and the children. Though I have tried being patient with her and even talked to her about this, it has not helped in solving the problem. Now the mere thought of going home from office to face an irritated wife seems daunting. Does Vastu Shastra have some cure for saving our relationship?

We men generally take our wives for granted. We expect them to be there for us, all the time and give us a warm welcome every time we return home from office. This self-centric approach of men does not take into account what the lady of the house may have gone through during the day. As long as she is warm and smiling, we are by her side, but the moment she starts to express herself in ways not to our liking, we walk out. This does not help matters and puts a severe strain on the relationship.

Your case is not peculiar and I have come across a lot of men with similar complaints. Before you put all the blame on your wife for spoiling the relationship, find out where the fault lies. Is your wife stressed about anything? Are the children giving her a hard time? Are you doing enough for her? Are you at least giving a sympathetic ear to her complaints? If you have analyzed the problem and have not found yourself wanting, it is time to search for a remedy outside.

Vastu Tips

Vastu Shastra identifies certain elements that may be negatively influencing your relationship. Since the arrangements within a house directly influences spousal relationships, it is important to assess them first. Look at the bedroom door. A patterned or carved door adversely affects the occupants of the bedroom. If you have such a door, replace it with a smooth-surfaced one, preferably made out of a single piece of wood. Also ensure that the furniture kept in the room does not have sharp edges like a table with pointed corners. If it does, ensure that no corner points towards the bed. It is best to opt for rounded furniture with curved smooth lines.

Protruding bookshelf is another source of strained relationship. Especially damaging is the open bookshelf, stretching from floor to the ceiling that directly faces the bed. It acts as knife slicing into the occupants of the room causing pain, disagreements and serious quarrels. If you have open shelves on any side of the bed, it is best to remove them totally. If that is not feasible then convert them into cupboards by affixing door panels on them. However, don't use mirrors or glass panes for this purpose as their reflection may create other problems, use solid wood instead. If this is also not possible, cover these shelves with curtains. Make these changes and return from office to be in the warm embrace of your wife!

Disinterested Husband

> I had been living with my boyfriend for the past one year till we decided to get married. We tied the knot last month. However, before we were married, I always found him fun loving and enjoyed his company, but this lasted only till our honeymoon. When we returned to our new flat, I found him taking less and less interest in me and, of late, has started distancing himself from me. I am sure he is not in any other relationship. But I am at a loss to find the reason for this

behaviour. Is there a Vastu remedy for my problem?

Marriage is different from living together. It is not necessarily better, but it is different. Both of you have different expectations from a spouse than from a live in partner or a lover. This is often based on expectations of what you saw of your parent's married life. Successful couples discuss in detail about their expectations from each other before they get committed in matrimony. If there is a serious disagreement – for example he wants kids and she doesn't – they consider all angles before tying the knot. After the wedding too, successful couples talk regularly to check their expectations of each other and if they clash, they keep their lines of communication wide open until they reach an understanding or an agreement

In your case, you must get to the bottom of why he is distancing himself from you. Are your lines of communications open or are you not open enough, making him suspicious? In your case, it seems that your husband is simply losing interest in you, since he is not accusing you of anything or remarking about your looks to make you feel guilty. So, discuss this matter of diminishing love with him, before you try out anything else. This way you will be able to reach out to him and find the best solution to your problem. In case he is not cooperative or is avoiding you, then the fault may lie in your new setting.

Vastu Tips

According to Vastu Shastra, love between newly-weds may wane because of the location of bedroom. Find out in which direction your bedroom lies. You, as a newly-wed couple, should always occupy a room to the north-west of the house and never in the south-east. In case you are staying in any other room, immediately shift into a north-west room to rejuvenate your love life.

Another thing that you should ensure for maintaining a happy, loving relationship with your husband is the correct position and direction of the bed. The south-west corner of the bedroom is most suitable for placing the bed. However, ensure that the foot of the bed doesn't directly face the door of the room. Also avoid sleeping under a beam hanging from the ceiling, as it causes marital disharmony.

Make sure that north east corner is not cluttered in any way. Indoor plants, white flower in the north corner and purple or the red rose in the south west corner of your bedroom would help in improving the relationship and to enjoy the ecstasies of love.

Unfaithful Husband

> I am in my mid-50s, having been married for the past 30 years. I recently discovered that my husband is having an affair with a younger woman and I'm devastated. When I confronted him, he termed it a one-night

> stand and promised it would never happen again, but I am not sure. I don't know what to do. Although, I don't want to leave him at this point in my life, my continuing to stay with him, despite knowing of his dalliance, may send out wrong signals. My husband doesn't understand why this 'little mischief' on his part upsets me so much. Is there a Vastu solution to my problem?

It appears that everything you say is based on fear. You are scared of forgiving your husband in case he cheats on you again. Scared of leaving him because the future seems unclear to you. Scared of staying with him in case it looks as if you are accepting his behaviour. You need to step aside from your fears and begin to concentrate on what you want in life. You have to take responsibility for your own happiness.

What do you want? Do you want to make your marriage work? Or do you want to be free of him and your marriage, to make your own future and find new love? If you want to leave, then go for it. Don't be fearful of how other people will respond. They are more understanding and will admire you for your determined choice. But if you want to stay, then you must put the past behind you and concentrate on building a good relationship with your husband to win him over.

Vastu Tips

Vastu has suggestions to restore fidelity in marriage. But before applying the remedial measures, find out what ails the house. If the house is T-shaped and located in the south-east of the plot, it causes division of good energies that may lead your spouse to 'look beyond'. Since it may not be possible to make a structural change, you could try and neutralise it by hanging a mirror at the junction.

Another reason of this dalliance is the existence of depression in the direction of the setting sun, that is, the west. This exposes the spouse to excessive negative energies that work against marriage. You must fill up this depression or, if not practical, hang a brass bell. Its vibrations would counter the effects of these negative energies.

A point connected to the above that encourages infidelity is the incorrect location of water bodies like pond, tank or swimming pool. A wrongly placed swimming pool causes infidelity and develops a roving eye in the men folk of the house. So, ensure that the pool is located only in the north-east and never towards the south-west of the house. Also, do not opt for a plot or a house that has a pond or a water tank in any direction other than the north-east.

Mirrors in the bedroom, which directly face the bed, are the main cause of marriages getting crowded. Generally, they encourage infidelity. The larger the mirrors, the more harmful they are to a marriage.

The most harmful are those covering the entire walls, causing discontentment in the couple and forcing them to look elsewhere for satisfaction. The best way to overcome this problem is to remove the mirrors completely from the bedroom. If this is not practical then hide them with a heavy drape and keep them covered throughout the night. Mirrors that are part of the dressing table should also not face the bed. So, adjust the dressing table accordingly.

In addition to mirrors, avoid anything in threes in your bedroom like candle stands, lights, curtains, chairs, pictures, etc., as they may attract a third person. Before this person appears physically, it is best to either add or remove one item in this trio to turn it into a single or double pair. Also, never display any kind of artificial flowers in the bedroom if you don't want your husband to have a roving eye. It encourages middle-aged or older husbands to develop a taste for younger women!

Too Fatigued for Each Other

> My husband and I both work, but by the time we get home, make dinner and spend time with the kids, we feel exhausted. It seems we never have any time for each other. And I feel that it is beginning to strain our relationship. Does Vastu Shastra have any suggestions?

The strain you are experiencing in your marriage is a prevalent problem for working parents. The relationship between you and your spouse is the cornerstone of your family's stability and happiness, so it is important to reconnect with your spouse. Though, children and work undoubtedly take much of your time, attention and energy, the trick is to avoid getting so immersed in these responsibilities that you neglect spending quality time with your spouse.

The best way to restore your togetherness is to take a break from your busy harried life and enjoy some time with your spouse alone, to talk, to laugh and to do the things you used to enjoy doing together when you were newly-weds. However, just ignoring your responsibilities is easier said than done; you have to make your spouse a priority and take conscious steps to create the right ambience for spending time together.

Vastu Tips

According to Vastu Shastra, the south and south-west corner of your house is where love reigns. Shift your bedroom to any of these directions to rejuvenate love, romance and family happiness. And never bring office work into this room! Computers or office files are a no no, since they generate conflicting energies. The reflecting screen of the computer acts much like a mirror and the files and folders contained within cause distractions that harms a loving relationship. So, don't let work come between the two of you or your relationship may cool off. In case, due to space constraints, you have to have your office in your bedroom, place a partition that separates your bed from your working area. This would help keep the energies inside the bedroom quiet and calm, heightening intimacy. As an added step, place a happy family photo in the south-west corner of your room.

Selfish Love

> My husband, though quite caring, is very selfish when it comes to intimacy. He doesn't seem to care for my needs and desires during our intimate moments and only works for the attainment of his own satisfaction. This adds to my frustration and makes me irritable. How can Vastu help us achieve a mutually fulfilling sexual relationship?

When reduced to basics, women need men to be romantic, caring, and loving. Men need women to be respectful, supportive, and loyal. They are the forces deeply rooted in the human personality. But this is just one side of the story. Millions of marriages are in trouble today because of the inability of both sexes to satisfy each other in bed. Perhaps the fundamental problem is one of selfishness. We are so intent on satisfying our own desires that we fail to recognise the longings of our partners.

This frustration in marriage, due to unsatisfying sex life, stems from a number of reasons that may be both physical and mental. However, as you say that your husband does not lack in performance but focuses more on his own fulfillment without caring for yours, may be because of a number of reasons and the fault may lie with you. It may be that you don't get aroused quickly enough. Many women take inordinately long to get aroused and fail to keep pace with their husbands. The result is lack of orgasm and frustration. To avoid this, it is best to discuss the matter openly with your husband. If he is caring, as you claim that he is, he will surely understand and will certainly do something about it. Drive home the point to him that the institution of marriage works best when we think less about ourselves and more about the ones we love. On the physical plane, if you are both normal, an extended foreplay may help you tide over this problem. Suggest this to your husband without appearing to be too knowledgeable about the subject!

Vastu Tips

Vastu Shastra can help you rejuvenate your flagging love life. As a first step, to get yourself in the right frame of mind for sex, create a romantic ambience in the bedroom. Place soft or pastel coloured lampshades with soft lighting in the south-west of the room and remove harsh lighting and spotlights as they dampen desire. Use pink bed sheets, slipping between them enhances intimacy and gets you quickly into the mood. This setting will fan your flames of desire and lead you towards an earth-shattering encounter, where you will certainly prove your husband's equal!

Real Red Rose in the south-west corner would really work miraculous in generating the powerful love energies.

❑

Chapter Three

Relationship between Parents and Children

"Dad, did you know what happened in my school today?" said Montu excitedly on finding his dad back from the office. "Later Montu, I am reading the newspaper," his dad snapped irritably, "Just keep my glass on the table, will you?" "Keep it yourself, I am busy!" snapped Montu and looked defiantly at his dad. This unexpected rebuff took dad unawares and infuriated him. He shouted, "How dare you disobey me, you rascal. I will show you life in no time." Dad gets up and Montu starts to run, only to get caught near the stairway. Two tight slaps across the face leaves Montu bawling his heart out. Hearing him cry, Montu's mother rushes into the room and looks accusingly at dad who by now had resumed his reading. "You are always after him," she complained, "Ever heard of anyone raising a hand on a teenager?" "Bah! Thirteen years is no age and this chap has the nerve of refusing me. Besides, I haven't hit him, I only drilled some sense into him. The fault actually lies with you. It is your pampering that is turning him into a spoilt brat." This irks Montu's mother and a heated exchange ensues, spoiling everybody's mood.

Why do parents and children display such behaviour? How can this growing rift with children be bridged to make them their parent's pet again? The key word for this befriending process is communication, talking, conversing, chatting or whatever else your like to call it. This exercise has been a part of our relationship with children right from the beginning, we taught them their first word. We told them their first bedtime story. However, somewhere along the line, we as parents, have lost touch with them. Why? Because we have stopped talking to them and are generally 'talking at them'. And that is why we are increasingly faced with Montu's type of reaction. The first thing to understand about communicating with your child is listening. While you are having a conversation with him or her, don't judge or preach, just listen.

Vastu Shastra lays great emphasis on togetherness, that is, finding quality time for one another within the family. It also suggests ways and means of building a strong bond between the parents and the children. I have come across a number of queries from worried mothers about their children that range from their not eating properly to going against their wishes. Adhering to the principles of Vastu has been able to solve these problems.

Fatigued Father

> My husband has recently taken up a high-stress job and its pressures have started to tell on him, which is interfering with our family life. My children are getting older and have started to notice. The other day my eldest daughter wanted to play with him, but was rebuffed, since he was too fatigued to play. I realise the strain my husband is under and understand his need to kick back and relax, but I am worried about the family's togetherness. Can Vastu help us having more quality time together?

It is not that your husband doesn't want to spend more time with the children, he is simply not able to because of his job. So, you need to redefine what family time should mean in the present scenario. With your husband totally immersed in a high-stress job and your kids growing, it is important to take advantage of the ordinary moments you find yourself together as a family. Teach your kids to take pleasure in these fleeting family interactions that infuse a feeling of togetherness. Regularly involve them in activities that you do with your husband like gardening, shopping, walking the dog, etc. For these interactions to be fun, it is important to tell your husband to retain a happy demeanour, irrespective of his hectic workday.

To help your husband de-stress, arrange for him to relax by doing activities together like watching television, reading, doing a puzzle, going for a walk, playing a game or doing something that gives pleasure to him and the family. This way the children will remain involved and will not pester him unnecessarily.

Vastu Tips

Vastu Shastrá can help your husband de-stress. The moment he returns from office, make him change from work clothes into ones he feels comfortable in. Ensure that he changes in the south-west corner of the bedroom as this direction bestows tranquility that will help him in cooling down. Let him have his privacy and don't let children pounce on him immediately on his arrival, as he may not be in a mood to entertain right away. Once he has changed, let him sit quietly in his favourite chair to watch the news or read the newspaper while he reacclimatizes to the home environment. Place his chair in the south-west portion of the living room so that he faces north-east. This direction helps in generating positive energies that help build strong relationships amongst the family members. Once he is relaxed, you can allow the kids to join him in tea and snacks. Ensure that your husband also eats and drinks facing the north-east. Try this and you will find your husband more open and loving towards others.

Working Mother

My husband works in the Middle East and visits us just once a year. To get rid of boredom, I have taken up a demanding marketing job. The problem is that my two sons, aged eight and 10, have to be left with the maidservant who picks them up from school and looks after them in my absence. However, every time I return home, I find them annoyed and quite destructive. I would like to give them all the attention that they deserve but I generally feel too tired after work. Can Vastu Shastra make my children happy?

The first question that you should ask yourself is whether you really need to continue with the job at this juncture when your kids are still small. If it is, your problem is the same as that of many single parents. Since you have taken up a job to use your talent and avoid boredom, it is creating a conflict within you, making you guilty. In case if it is possible, opt for a little less demanding job that gives you more time with the kids.

If you feel you have no choice but to continue in the same job, do not berate yourself for what you don't or can't do. Chalk out a routine and let your children adapt to it and make sure your kids are well cared for in your absence. Be the best mother you can be for your kids make yourself available to them as much as you can. In your case, it will be the quality of time rather won the quantity that will make the difference. Give extra love and care to your kids at home on your return from office and always listen to their complaints. It may be that the maidservant is giving them a hard time. Ensure that you have at least one meal together. Plan outings on your holidays and encourage the kids to speak to their father over the telephone, whenever possible. If you plan well, these problems will eventually get sorted out in your favour.

Vastu Tips

According to Vastu Shastra, the best place for meeting in a house is the dining room where one gets a chance to talk to one another over meals. This strengthens the family bond and takes loneliness away. If possible locate the dining room in the west and set it up in such a manner that you feel like spending time there. You can create a zone of tranquility by placing a couch or a settee with cushions along with a small side table near the north-east corner of the dining room. If you are short of space and can't place any furniture, display a photo of someone you respect or place a hanging plant, such as basil. Locate the dining table in the west or east of the room. The east, being the direction of enlightenment, motivates stimulating conversation and west provides peace. Make these changes and find your kids well adjusted, happy and bubbling with life.

Lazy Teenager

I have a 16-year old school-going daughter, who just likes to sit around and never helps me with the housework, even in her spare time. This attitude of hers makes me mad and we often end up fighting. Is there a Vastu cure for making her responsible?

Life is much easier in a family when there is a spirit of cooperation. What your daughter is displaying is not uncommon. It would have been ideal if you had taught her to be responsible from the very beginning. Many parents do everything for their children, thus instilling the idea at an early age that if they don't do it, someone else will. This gives a wrong signal to the child.

It is not that children don't want to help; they do, but they want to play a meaningful part in the functioning of the family and not just be ordered around all the time. Your effort should be to involve your daughter in family decisions. This will give her a sense of contributing to the betterment and welfare of the family and infuse her with a spirit of cooperation. Give her time to express her feelings. In the rush of life, we need to take time to listen to the child. An extra few minutes may be all she needs to get her to cooperate. Children love to help plan, organise, and carry out family decisions. Respect the opinions and feelings of your daughter. Help her feel like her opinions count even when a decision other than hers' is taken. Once a decision has been reached, give some responsibility to her for carrying out those decisions. She will be happier knowing that she is contributing towards a family decision. Finally, don't forget to praise her when you see her putting an effort to cooperate. This guarantees future cooperation.

Vastu Tips

Vastu Shastra lays emphasis on the location and arrangement of children's room to get them in the right frame of mind for cooperation. If these are ideal, children will be obedient, more open to suggestions and more inclined to cooperate. Children have impressionable minds and need a nurturing environment. Vastu Shastra recognizes this fact and recommends north, east, north-east or north-west of the house as the most ideal location for children's room. It may also be located in the south-east, but should never be in south or southwest. Some Vastu experts even suggest north-west direction as ideal for girls and south-east for boys. To help a child become calmer and more caring, paint the walls white or light shades of blue, pink or orange. Avoid dark colours since they make the children dull and self-centred. Making these changes will make your daughter in helping you out around the house.

Also putting green trees picture or the picture/ calendar showing good greenery in her room would give birth to the good and productive ideas to her. She will become prudent, cool and cooperative.

Poor Performance in School

My son, studying in 10th standard, is consistently under performing in school,

> though he used to be good in studies previously. He continues to earn low grades despite all our support. No amount of advice or threats has forced him to improve his class performance. This is straining our loving relationship with him. Is there a Vastu solution to this problem?

This problem besets most families where children, who were initially good in studies, become underachievers despite all help rendered to them in the form of private tutors and exclusive study rooms. A 10th standard kid needs to be tackled tactfully, since threats will only make him resent you. As a first step, have faith in your child. He needs to be offered positive reinforcements. If he needs help with his homework, offer suggestions to help him find the information himself. Tell him that you have confidence in his ability to complete the work all by himself. When your child listens to you and does what you ask promptly, praise him and tell him how much you appreciate his actions. Also, never criticize him in front of others. This will go a long way in building his self-esteem and consequently motivate him to prove his worth. Once his studies improve, he will automatically earn appreciation from all, improving his relationships with others.

Vastu Tips

According to Vastu Shastra, the problem faced by most students as regards their grades, generally lies in the location of the study room and the arrangements within. Wrongly placed study room or incorrect placement of components within, negatively influences the child and strains his relationships with others. On the other hand, an ideally located study room contributes tremendously to the acquisition of knowledge and motivates the individual to become an effective member of the family, mending relationships.

Ideally, locate the study room in the north, north-east or east of the house. These directions improve the powers of learning and retention in students. East is particularly good, since it is the direction of inspiration and enlightenment. West, especially between west and south-west, is also acceptable. However, locating the study room in the north-west, which belongs to the realm of air and movement, is likely to make the students restless, unfocussed and indecisive.

The location of study table within the study room is also important. Locate it in the south or west, especially if the table is heavy. However, some suggest north-east portion of the room as the most ideal, since it inculcates optimism, sharp wit and determination to achieve goals in children.

A square table of an appropriate size, that is, neither too big nor too small, is best suited for study table. A large table weakens the grasping power of the student and reduces his working capacity, whereas a small table puts pressure on him leading to depression. If possible, don't let the table face the door, as whatever is learnt slips out. Best is to sit with the back towards the door. This enhances learning abilities and capacity for retention. Also, ensure that the study table never touches the wall and is placed at least four inches away from it. This helps the student in quick grasp of the material and longer retention. Those who don't have a separate study room can place their study table in their bedroom, but it should adhere to the same Vastu principles.

Once you take these steps, your child will certainly become an achiever again and will automatically improve his relationships with everyone.

Balancing Family and Profession

> I am a bachelor staying with my parents and my unmarried sister, and have had to struggle very hard to make a career for myself. Since my parents are dependent upon me, I am facing financial problems too. For job security and to enhance my income, I decided to pursue a management course. But the problem is that the course requires commitment, time and effort. As a result, I am not able to devote time to my family. This is making them very unhappy. The course will last for two more years and I need to make up my mind whether I should complete the course or not. I need my family

to cooperate to get this professional degree. How can Vastu help me in making them understand that I am taking the course for the good of the family and not for fun?

You need to balance your professional and family life properly. Many people are caught in such a cleft and find it difficult to manage both the lives. Your desire is to rise in one's career along with studying to qualify for a better future. On the other hand, your family is seeking your time. The demands of both are time and energy consuming and the problem is of managing things satisfactorily. It is best to talk things over with your family and make them understand the demands of work and study. Let them know why you are studying and how this would contribute to your family's betterment in the future. Then prioritize all your activities. When one activity needs time and energy, put the other two on the backburner. Then, take up the next task. Attend to all the needs, but one at a time! This will help prove that you are not neglecting anyone. Your family will wait for their turn more willingly when you are attending to the other two.

The most important thing here is to win the family's confidence for what you are doing and then watch all your problems disappear. Remember that no family wants to discourage its bread earner to move ahead professionally.

Vastu Tips

Indoor plant in the kitchen and a photo of Golden Temple or any religious calendar or the photograph of Pole situated near the bank of a river on the south vest wall of the drawing room would help them in increasing the understanding level among the family members and creating a healthy and powerful atmosphere.

❑

Chapter Four

Relationship with Elders of the Family

"Dadaji, don't take that chair. I want to sit on it to do my homework," snapped Anil, at his grandfather. "Why don't you take some other chair, you know I always sit on this chair," replied his grandfather. Anil said nothing, got up and went inside. "What?" Anil's mother sounded aghast, "he did not allow you to sit where you wanted. What does he think of himself? Just hanging around uselessly and poking nose in other people's affairs, that's all he does the whole day. Wait till I tell your dad."

"Papaji, why didn't you let Anil sit wherever he wanted to? His studies are getting unnecessarily disturbed. If you wanted to sit, you could have sat on the sofa." Anil's daddy was very categorical and his papa thought better than to reply. Dadaji had been enduring his grandson's rude behaviour for quite sometime now. He knew that this brat was being encouraged by her mother, but felt powerless to do anything about it. With his own son firmly in the grip of his daughter-in-law, he was afraid to make an issue of small things since he had to stay with them. At 78 this widower had no one else to turn to.

Infirm a with weakening faculties, he had no choice but to cares on existing in this environment, till the very end.

This certainly is not a unique scenario. Today, there are families where it is not unusual to see even four living generations co-existing side by side instead of the three With the advancement of medicine and health care, many elders have started experiencing full lives, several decades past 60, and are quite capable of enjoying a robust existence till the end. However, their relationship with others at home on a day-to-day basis is entirely a different issue. Elders, as they advance in age, become more sensitive to the opinions of others. They want to help in their own way but their help around the house is misconstrued as hindrance. Their say in running the house is interpreted as meddling in household affairs.

For family members too, it becomes a problem to handle elders tactfully. If you disturb their routine due to unavoidable circumstances, they take it as a personal affront. If you want to help them from boredom by suggesting some work around the house, they think they are being ordered around. Their merely sitting around without work but involving themselves in the day-to day affairs of the house seems an outright interference to the other members of the family. Furthermore, if they don't contribute towards the running of the house or their own upkeep, they seem a burden to the family. And if, by any chance, the house belongs to the elders that you are hoping to inherit, then you face another set of complications.

Vastu Shastra suggests ways to ease the problems arising out of such relationships in a joint family. If the principles of Vastu are applied sincerely, they not only help the elders adjust better, but also persuade a grudging household to lovingly accept them.

Lonely Father

> My mother died two years ago and it left my father feeling quite lonely. Though we take good care of him, we have observed that time has not healed his loss and he still feels quite lonesome without her. Though he puts up a brave front on the outside, he is no more his old jovial self. Suspecting depression, I have shown him to a few doctors but they don't recommend any medication. Can Vastu Shastra help him in overcoming this grief

Death, especially of a wife, is a tragic event. Having spent a good part of one's life with her, through all the ups and downs, one is bound to develop a special bond of love. If she leaves one's side at this juncture, the loss becomes most pronounced and may come as a shock, particularly if it is sudden. Though most old people prepare themselves for this eventuality, there are a few who still can't get over the trauma of loss. It seems your father is still in a state of shock and is finding no one to share his grief with. You need to make him snap out of it and bring him to his old jovial self again.

As a first step, make a happy environment in the house, which is easier said than done! However, you can ensure that lines of communication between you father and your family, particularly your wife, remain open throughout. You will have to explain to them even elders need a sympathetic ear at times. Tell not to get irked by his ways and accept him as he is. This step will help form a loving bond between him and the family.and divert his mind from whatever troubling him. Another step that you can take is to involve him in some project or the other. Resident Welfare Association offers great opportunities to do useful work for the society and provides a chance for making friends. Discuss this option with your father and introduce him to the Association. Your encouragement will certainly go a long way in helping him find a new meaning in life.

Vastu Tips

Though Vastu Shastra cannot grant instant happiness to your father, it suggests certain steps by which you can create a happy and healthy environment at home. Vastu Shastra lays stress on the influence of natural light on the moods of individuals. Ensure that your father's room is adequately lit. Make it a point to regularly open all doors and windows in the morning to admit sunlight and fresh air. Living in darkness or in a place where there is no natural light is most unhealthy. Even scientifically it has been shown that many people suffer from clinical depression during long, dark winter months. If the room does not have access to the outside then always leave a light on during the day.

Ensure blue bulb is on when he goes to sleep.

Attention Seeking Mother-in-law

> My aged, widowed mother-in-law is staying with us and is always complaining. Whenever I make any new dish, she insists that she could have prepared it better, but when I invite her to cook, she doesn't want to shake a finger. When she finds the family's attention shifting from her, she starts complaining about her health imagining herself afflicted with some dreaded disease even though she hates doctors. This attitude of hers gets me all worked up and is putting a strain on our relationships. Is there Vastu way out of this problem?

Mothers-in-law in any home are a force to reckon with. However, most mellow down with time and, as old catches up with them, they slowly start getting dependent on their daughters-in-law. In a few case, these women, due to some insecurity, want to remain the centre of attention of the household. In your case, it seems your widowed mother-in-law is craving for love and attention. So, the first thing is to change her attitude by subtly emphasizing that she will be showered with equal love and attention as other members of the family. As you attempt to change her outlook, she may react in different ways—indifferent, at best or outright rude, at worst. However, don't get deterred, once she grasps the sincerity of your intentions, she will appreciate your even-handedness and will work towards strengthening the loving bond with you.

You can also win her over by love. However, in this, the main problem is that of ego. Your first reaction would be why should you approach her, why can't she take the initiative? As a more enlightened being, you should swallow your pride and make the first move, as a mark of respect for the elderly. Once this love between your mother-in-law and the family grows, you will feel a kind of warmth you have never felt before.

Vastu Tips

One of the main culprits contributing towards lack cohesion and differing viewpoints in a household cluttering of utensils in the kitchen. This diffuses the harmony, which is normally generated when you eat together. To restore a harmonious balance amongst the family members and especially between the family and your mother-in-law, never let the utensils lie around kitchen. Always arrange them properly in racks every time they are washed. This will help mend every relations at home.

Take a look at your mother-in-law's bedroom. Is there a light bulb hanging without a shade? Harsh light from a naked bulb creates tension, spoiling relationships and may even cause ill health. Ensure that all naked bulbs in her room are covered with lampshades. You can also use a dimmer to diffuse bright lights.

Keep an indoor plant in the kitchen in the east corner preferably or any where else wherever it is possible. It will help in maintaining good health of all the family members and create a healthy environment and relationship among the family members.

Always Fearing the Worst

> We are an issueless septuagenarian couple and my husband is eight years my senior. My love for him has grown over the years in our 50 years of marriage. Lately, I have started suffering from bad thoughts. I am always thinking what will happen to me if my husband dies. It has taken the form of anxiety, so much so that even if my husband comes in late from his morning walk, I fear the worst. If he is sleeping and does not move, I go and shake him awake just to find out if he is still alive. I just can't get rid of these thoughts and it is making our life miserable. Is there a Vastu cure for me?

According to the psychiatrists, such behaviour is directly attributed to one's experiences in life. Can you recall any incident that may have happened to make you insecure about your husband? Or does he have a health problem that requires attention? If so, look into the matter and get him investigated. If you are insecure because of financial reasons, knowing nothing about money matters, and are afraid you won't know how to fend for yourself after he goes, it is best to face your fears and openly discuss the issues with him. Especially find out what plans and investments he has made. If no such incident has taken place, then your problem is more in the nature of obsessive thought, which is creating unnecessary fear and panic in your mind. Don't worry but don't try to run away from your thoughts either. The more you run away, the more you will think about them. Try and involve yourself in activities that engage you, diverting your mind away from bad thoughts. If things don't get better, take recourse to other forms of remedy.

Vastu Tips

According to Vastu Shastra, insecurity stems from a fault either in the construction of the house or the arrangements within. Take a look at your bedroom. If its north-east corner is cut then it may be responsible for your insecurity. North contributes towards mental stability, being the direction of wisdom, and east, wealth and life. Any deficiency in these directions is bound to affect the mental state of the individual. The remedy is to hang a small mirror on the wall towards the cut end of the room to "extend the energy zone.

In case the north-east corner of your room is perfect, take a look at the alignment of your beds. They should preferably lie along north-south, with their heads towards the south. Never sleep with your head towards the north since your head being the north of the body repels the magnetic north, putting pressure on your mind, making you feel nervous and insecure. As a rule, always sleep with your with your head towards the south or east. These steps will go a long way in curing you of your insecurities.

Alcoholic Elder

> My 70-year old uncle is a retired army officer and a confirmed bachelor. He stays in a separate house near us. The problem is that he drinks excessively and creates a ruckus that disturbs the peace and tranquility of the neighbourhood. It has now begun to influence my children adversely. No amount of advice has made him give up this habit. Can Vastu help him get rid of the problem?

Alcohol abuse, coupled with aggressive behaviour, is a problem that can affect people of any age. It is evident that your uncle gave up trying to control his drinking a long time back to arrive at this stage. The reason is that no problem drinker will ever admit that he doesn't know how to drink safely, that he is sick.

Your uncle suffers from the same feelings of guilt, loneliness and hopelessness that are displayed by confirmed drinkers. He is afflicted with the disease of alcoholism that fuels his violent nature.

It seems a case of neglect on your part too, to let this habit reach such a stage. You only woke up once your own children started getting affected. Had you taken timely action this situation would have been contained in the initial stages itself. Remember, alcoholism is an illness, a 'progressive' illness, which can never be cured which, like some other diseases, 'can' be arrested. This illness represents a combination of physical sensitivity to alcohol and a mental obsession drinking, which cannot be broken by will-power alone.

Recognizing that there is a problem is the first towards recovering from problem drinking. If you think that your uncle is an alcoholic, speak to him and let him acknowledge his problem openly. Advise him to stay away from people who encourage drinking alcohol or who preach that a drinking problem is a problem of weak will. Depending upon the degree of alcohol dependency, it will not be a bad idea to seek professional help.

Vastu Tips

Vastu Shastra maintains that aggressiveness and addictions are a result of fluctuations of energy levels within a house. For example, if the floor levels in the south-west of your uncle's house are lower than those in the north-east, his health and energy levels drain out, making him more prone to violence and addictions. For a remedy to this fault, try and see if you can raise the lower levels to equalize the balance. If not, then you must place heavy objects in the south-west to compensate for higher north-east.

Similarly, ensure that the boundary wall along the north is lower than that in the south. Not doing this will constantly drain the energy levels, depleting the person of the vital *prana*, which restores health. The body in order to restore the depletion may become addicted to alcohol or drugs. If this fault lies in your uncle's house, re-establish the balance by raising the southern wall either with concrete or a bamboo fence. If either is impossible, run a copper or silver wire across the width of the wall. This remedy will bring about a balance in energies, persuading your uncle to give up on his addiction and restrain his aggressiveness.

❑

Part II
Relationships Outside the Family

PART TWO

Relationships Outside the Family

"Life consists not in holding good cards but in playing those you hold well."

– Josh Billings

Relationships within a family are a private affair of its members and any problems arising within can be dealt with in the exclusivity of the home. However, relationships outside the family come directly under the scrutiny of all and have been regarded as one of the most difficult areas of human life. Be it our relationships with lovers, friends or neighbours, it takes an effort to keep them healthy and ticking. These people, after our own immediate family members, may become a source of our deepest anxieties, fears, insecurities, unhappiness or pain, as indeed of joy, love, support, comfort, guidance and even liberation.

We are forced to spend so much time on nurturing our relationships outside the family because we consider them central to our happiness and self esteem. In fact, they can make or break us by enhancing or tarnishing our reputation and image in the society. If we can master the secret to getting them right, we may not only prevent much unhappiness, but also actually derive a good deal of contentment.

And we may finally find a way to be at peace with ourselves and with others.

However, maintaining healthy relationships outside the family is easier said than done. These relationships are often intricate labyrinths in which every mistake gets magnified, every error multiplied until we find ourselves completely lost, helpless, confused and even devastated. To approach this complex human problem we must realise that no relationship is simple or can be taken for granted. It needs a lot of work, patience tolerance and compassion. The key is to work towards removing insecurities and suspicions that may crop up from time to time. Indeed it is our own likes and dislikes and our inability to overlook the shortcomings that cause many of our problems in relationship.

To earn respect and love of those around us, we need to learn to love and care. If we ourselves are dry and depleted within, how can we expect others to quench our thirst? In most cases, we seek completion, fullness and adequacy through others, whereas we ourselves are not prepared to give it to them. The result? Disappointment with lovers, friends, neighbours and all other acquaintances with whom we come in contact in our daily lives. There are times when some relationships seem difficult or impossible and cannot be avoided or ignored. In such cases, instead of wishing away the person that cannot be wished away, we should train ourselves to deal with him or her with a joyou detachment, rather than a sorrowful resistance. Or we should mend our relationships through the age-old science of Vastu Shastra.

To strengthen our bonds with our lovers, friends neighbours, Vastu Shastra emphasizes correct layout and construction of the house and the arrangement within. According to it, adherence to the Vastu can not only accord harmony to the occupants but also confer happy relationships, enhancing friendship. Not only would you enrich yourself but also succeed in your quest for fulfillment. Let us take a look at the various relationships outside the house and what Vastu Shastra recommends for improving them.

❑

Chapter Five

Relationship with Lovers

From the expression on Akhil's face, Simi knew that the love bug had bitten him. She herself was attracted to him the moment she saw him. This was only their first meeting and that too with friends. It was love at first sight! There was little doubt in their young minds that they were made for each other. And since that day, they began to see each other regularly. As their love blossomed and their mutual trust strengthened, the intimacy between them broke all bounds. Then one fine day the hour of reckoning came.

"Akhil, I think I am pregnant," Simi announced to a stunned Akhil. "*How*?" was all that he could blurt out, knowing very well that he was responsible. This shocking news was very disturbing for Akhil and from that day, he started avoiding Simi. Seeing her beloved behaving in this way panicked Simi who did not know how to handle the situation. She tried to approach him. but was politely shown the door with all kinds of excuses. Her plight seemed no better than a Hindi film's unwed mother. As the lovechild grew in her womb, she was left with no choice but to tell her mother. The moment she did that, all hell broke lose. Her father immediately disowned her and her mother cried heart out. Simi could never imagine that a little negligence on her part would result in this calamity. She felt betrayed by her boyfriend and was saddened by the way she was treated at home. She had never imagined that her fairytale relationship would end so tragically.

Most Young lovers base their idea of true love on children's fairy tales in which finding prince charming enchanting princess always leads to living happily ever after. Movies often portray this same storybook image – that falling in love is really just that: falling in love, going out of control, devoted towards the beloved who is meant to be with you and you alone.

But for most mortals, striving for such ideals in the real world is unrealistic and, more often than not, leaves them unfulfilled or let down. Staying in love takes continual work and patience and demands practical considerations, even though they might seem utterly unromantic in the context of the fairytale. Couples who have healthy relationships find ways of strengthening their bonds by working together at it. This certainly indicates true love.

If you are a victim of love gone awry or want to play it safe and prevent setbacks, Vastu Shastra can show you the way. I have reproduced certain live situations with suggested Vastu remedies. Take their help in resolving your problems and bask in the warm glow of togetherness.

Differing Religions

> Just two months after joining my new office, I fell for the most handsome man in the office. He also fully reciprocated my attention and we have been going steady since. He is intelligent, hardworking and cares a lot about me. I have decided to marry him but there is a problem. He is a Muslim, whereas I am a Hindu Brahmin. How can we tie the knot without upsetting our respective families?

Overcoming religious differences and having the strength to tackle the complications arising out of it is the ultimate example of true love and devotion. If we are able to cross the hurdles put up by the respective families, then you are sure to have your way. You show remember that for winning over the family, you have to adapt yourself totally to their way of thinking. You an bride-to-be must keep your lines of communication open with your would be in-laws. In this way, you will be one-to-one with them and will be able to prevent them from swaying to the tune of rumor mongers within the family, whose sole aim generally is to misguide. Your sincere efforts will allow them to know you better softening them up and strengthening your case. Similarly, encourage your would be husband to introduce himself to your family in a subtle manner. You can make him a part of your friends' circle in which you also invite your brother and introduce them to each other.

In the end, remember that a committed couple can survive in the most hostile environment. If you consider only the difficulties, you would have nothing; but if you see past them, you would have everything that matters. Compromise remains the magic word in this union.

Vastu Tips

Vastu Shastra does not discriminate against religions. For Vastu Purush, what matters is the structure of building. That is why there is no differentiation in location and setting of the prayer room based on religions. It is as inviting for Muslims, as it is for Christians or Hindus.

To enhance religious sentiments in a household, locate the prayer room in the north-east. Ensure that this corner is not cluttered and have access to sunlight and air. When setting up the prayer room in addition to displaying the images of Gods, keep the *Ramayana* and the *Koran* next to each other. This helps boost religious tolerance in the occupants of the house. Furthermore, to make yourself acceptable to the respective families, participate in Hindu and Muslim festivals and celebrate them with full gusto. This will strengthen family bonds and will help you ease into their fold. And they too, at their end, will start considering you as one of their own.

Keep a red rose in the crystal bowl or the glass half filled with water in the west corner of your bed room would help in bringing cheers and positive energies on the desired end.

Haunted by Past Trauma

> I had divorced my husband two years ago, since he was involved in some other relationship. Presently, I am single and working in a big firm. For some time, I have been noticing that one of my male colleagues is showing great interest in me. Though I like all the attention, I find it difficult to reciprocate; as I am reminded of my previous marriage and the hurt I have been put through. How can Vastu help me to let bygones be bygones and encourage me to get on with life?

It is hard to regain a sense of trust after a broken marriage. This feeling of uneasiness can cast a cloud over subsequent relationships, making you anxious about your ability to find love once again. You would do well to keep in mind that the reasons why some relationships don't last are as varied as the nature of people. In many cases, partners simply grow an because they have grown and changed as individuals, and seek different and more fulfilling opportunities for love.

You may very well ask whether humans are capable of staying in love. The answer is that they are, as there are people around us, who love and care deeply for each other. It is truly said 'better to have loved and lost, than never to have loved at all.' It would be best for you to consider your previous marriage, however traumatic, as a lesson that should not be repeated in your future relationship. Instead of nurturing your own heartache and steering away from relationship that seems to beckon you, take concrete steps to pick up the threads of your love life and start afresh. Go all out to reciprocate the attention of this colleague of yours, for all you know, true love might be waiting for you just around the corner!

Vastu Tips

In your situation, there is a need to turn on your charm to give positive signals to your male colleague. Vastu recommends a number of things you can do to enhance your allure and strengthen your love. But first, you have to cut your ties with the past. Throw out old love letters, furniture, trinkets, gifts and dried flowers from what was once a happy relationship. This will help you start afresh.

To attract mature relationship, remove stuffed animals, games and dolls. This is all girlie stuff that takes out the seriousness in a relationship. Also remove items that make you stray from your goal of cultivating relationship, such as exercise equipment, work-related items, laundry and television from your love area. Take these steps and find a partner of your dreams!

Also remove all sadistic pictures or calendars from your house.

Keep two rose flowers in the half filled glasses or the crystal bowls in the north and west corners of your house or the room to enhance the positive energies and to experience good results on the personal, emotional and love fronts. Also make sure there is no clutter in the north corner of your room.

Wear pink colours and try to get the walls of your room painted in pink. This will help in raising the levels of energy on the love end.

Age Difference

> Recently, my sister introduced me to a girl, her friend, who had just passed out of college. She was the most beautiful being I had ever laid my eyes on and I was drawn to her like a moth to an open flame. Since then, we had gone out a couple of times, but always accompanied by my family. Till now, I never had a chance to take her out alone. The problem is she is 10 years younger to me and this age difference makes me pretty uncomfortable. Although my friends say it is love that matters and nothing else, I am not sure. What would Vastu Shastra recommend for such a relationship?

You say you have been out with her just a couple of times and that too with the family, which means that you two haven't really interacted on a one-to-one basis. Your discomfort regarding the age difference may not be totally unfounded. An age difference of 10 years may not show now if the girl is mature enough and you are 'young' at heart, but it may matter later, especial compatibility is an issue. But love and age are not only factors. You should also find out what kind of person the girl is, her likes, dislikes, expectations relationship and so on. If you are looking at the prac tical aspect of a relationship, it is important to know if her interests and attitudes are somewhat similar to your. There are other factors too, which you need to explore like educational and family background. Once you are convinced on the compatibility issue, you can go ahead with your marriage plans.

Vastu Tips

The situation that you are in requires you to balance the male-female energies in your home to attract the girl you love. Since you are much older than her, you need to reduce female symbols at home. If feminine energy dominates a house or apartment, women visiting, it will have difficulty in having successful relationship with a man. Further, where rooms are cold, without pets and with complete absence of music, feminine energy overpowers the masculine force. This imbalance affects the social life negatively and a bachelor staying in such surroundings finds it hard to get the girl of his choice. So, remove dark-coloured paintings and brighten dim lights throughout the house and arrange your house with a good mixture of both male and female energies. Let feminine blues and blacks remain introduce masculine reds and yellows as well. Make your house as bright as possible. Also, it will be an added advantage if you hang the picture of your belove your room, that is, if you want to make her your lifemate.

School Crush

> I am head over heels in love with a guy in my school. Though I have been playing hard to get him, it doesn't seem to be working. Can Vastu Shastra help me?

Be honest and be yourself, which essentially means, be true to yourself. Ask yourself if you really love this guy or is it just a passing infatuation. Never let people talk you in doing things you don't want to do and don't let go of your values just to make someone else like you.

Also, when you play hard to get games, you are really not being honest. It doesn't mean that when you have a crush on someone, you tell it to them or start expressing your love for them. For your boyfriend not reacting to you, there is a possibility that you are playing this game a bit too well and he feels that you aren't interested in him. He may even have labelled you as arrogant.

With your young and impressionable mind, take time out to assess whether this guy is really for you. Do you really need him to make you happy? Look for someone who has the same values as you, who makes you feel good and with whom you can enjoy yourself. If you are certain that he is the right person for you, play a little less hard to get and see him home onto you like a bee to a flower!

Vastu Tips

To attract the boy of your dreams, it is important that you make some changes as per Vastu recommendations. For starters, remove all sharp angled objects and furniture from your room as their sharp edges poke into persons, keeping people you attract at bay. Also, throw away the cactus.

Pink is the color of love and pink-coloured stuff actually help hold love energy for you. Wear pink, even a hint of it will suffice. Introduce pink in your room, anything that is pink helps.

Shy Boyfriend

> I have a boyfriend in school who is gentle but quite shy. Though we have been meeting regularly for over a month now, he still hesitates in opening up with me and seems a bit of an introvert. He doesn't express his feelings at all which sometimes makes me wonder if he really loves me. Is there a Vastu cure to make him express his emotions?

School can be a very awkward time for both boys and girls, especially when they are in their teens. A lot of changes are just beginning to take place in emotions, thoughts and body. Even if your boyfriend was outgoing before, he could very well become shy and introspective in his teens. A month is not really long enough for meeting regularly and he may not feel comfortable in expressing his feelings within this short span of time. He may still be anxious about your opinion of him and may be worried if you are going to break up with him.

There could be certain other problems to make him reserved, like family problems, problem with his studies, and so on. The best way out of this situation is to ask him frankly what is on his mind and reassure regarding his fears. Forcing him to open up may scare him away, but your assurance that you can be trusted with whatever is on his mind and your caring attitude will help strengthen the bond of trust between you andhelp him become more communicative. However, you should continue to express your thoughts and feelings to him as before and let him know what he means to you. Then maybe he will feel more comfortable in opening up to you.!

Vastu Tips

You should bring your boyfriend out of his shell, gently and lovingly. For this, there is a need for you to energize your space, that is, wherever you two meet. Vastu suggests decorating your room with vibrant colours in combinations of red with green or yellow. Avoid blacks and blues. This will encourage him to converse. If you are meeting outside the school premises then you can stimulate him by valentine cards or other symbols of love and romance. You can also carry the universal expression of love on your person in the form of roses and peonies that is sure to inspire him to express himself. It is not necessary to use real roses; ones made from silk would do as well since they will never fade! But real rose would always do well.

The Comparison Game

> We are two friends studying in the same college. We both have boyfriends. Though mine is nice and does my bidding, I find my friend enjoying more than me with her boyfriend. This sometimes makes me question my relationship with my boyfriend. Is there a Vastu cure to make my love life as good as that of my girlfriend?

In an interview conducted recently, one group of people were asked to first describe an unhappy couple they know of and then describe their own relationship, and another group was asked to first describe a happy couple and then describe their own relationship. It was found that the former were 19 per cent more like describe their relationship as perfect than the latter.

It is natural that when we see a friend enjoying seemingly wonderful relationship, we begin to question our own. However, it is best not to play the comparison game. Evaluate your relationship based on your own needs and not on the relationship success of those around you. Remember, a relationship is not commodity like a DVD or a washing machine that can be replaced if it stops meeting your needs. If you treat your relationship as a product, you will certainly wonder why you can't trade it for a better one. If you start comparing your partner to others, you undermine what you have for what probably doesn't exist. After all, marketing is about making us dislike what we have and think what someone else has, is better.

Vastu Tips

There is a possibility that the problem you are facing may be caused by the mirrors in your house. According to Vastu Shastra, if your dressing mirror is not long enough and cuts the reflection of the body, it creates jarring energy, as you are unable to have the whole view of yourself. To get the full picture of who you are, your self-image is very important. This will infuse confidence in you, since your mental and physical well-being depends on it. So, to cure your condition, it is important to replace the smaller mirror with a full length one that should not only show the full body but shows it clearly and undistorted.

Problem Friends

> My problem is my boyfriend's friends. They are immature, drink too much and make disgusting, sexist comments. At first, I tried to cope with their behavior, but now I just can't take it and have complained about it to my boyfriend. He tells me to ignore them, but I don't think I can anymore. Can Vastu help my boyfriend get rid of them?

If these immature boys are your boyfriend's only friends, then may be you should help him make some new ones. Forget about nagging him or creating scenes that force him to choose between you and them. Instead, introduce him to new people. Why not encourage him to get to know your friends, for example? Invite them and their partners for drinks or dinner. Ask your coworkers to meet up for happy hour, and see to it that your boyfriend comes too. Building a new social life together won't happen overnight, since good things never do. But if you start the ball rolling, it will gather its own momentum. In the end, he will find himself eased into a social scene that happens to suit you both. However, if your efforts fail, it may be time to ask yourself what a kind of guy he is who chooses to be close with a bunch of alcoholic, sexist losers. It could simply be that these guys have a long history together or you may realize that the person you love is not much different from the company he keeps.

Vastu Tips

The need of the hour is to keep yourself away from frustration and maintain a positive outlook in life. This positiveness will help you to help your boyfriend out of the rut he is presently in. To always maintain a positive state of mind, Vastu Shastra recommends the technique of creative visualisation through meditation. Close your eyes and fix your consciousness on an image. It should be the image of your personal God or any pleasant object. Hold the image of your dream in your mind's eye. Now imagine what you desire is happening. Live it in the present so that you believe it has actually come to pass. Repeat this exercise daily or even twice a day. There is some evidence to show that the energy waves released by our mind attract the kind of time, space and events we expect in our lives. This process will surely help you cope up with the people you dislike and will also help draw away your boyfriend from them.

❑

Chapter Six

Relationship with Friends

"Kanchan, I really think you were quite rude to Hemant. All he said was you were looking great," complained Monica. "Monica, I don't like your boyfriend. He is always sarcastic. Didn't you see the way he complimented me? As if he was mocking at me," retorted Kanchan. And thus ensued a long and heated argument that left a bad taste in the mouths of both the girls.

Monica had known Kanchan from her school days. Since they had taken admission in the same college on their passing out from school, their earlier acquaintance had turned into close friendship. However, college life saw them expanding their circles and soon Monica was going steady with Hemant. This development was not to Kanchan's liking and she secretly started resenting Monica for her prize catch, since Hemant was much sought after by all the girls in the college. As Kanchan's envy grew, it started taking the form of frequent arguments and their once solid friendship started developing cracks. The day was not far when they would part ways.

A little competition between friends is common and healthy, as long as it's acknowledged, mutual and energizing to the relationship. Friendly rivalry can create inspiration, encouragement, and support. However, friendship fall-outs may become traumatic, since we don't generally expect conflict with friends. We love them and need them. They are as important as family, if not more, which is why we dread falling our friends.

Vastu Shastra acknowledges the importance of friendship and suggests remedies for broken friendships I have compiled a few problems on relationship with friends and their Vastu solutions. Try and apply these to your situations and see your friendship bloom.

Healthy Competition

> My best friend and I are university athletes. We are both long distance runners capable of beating each other on any given day. However, during recent trials for the marathon, I failed to qualify, whereas my friend made it into the team. This has embittered me and made me quite envious, but I do not want to spoil our friendship. Is there a Vastu cure to help me tide over this setback?

Any person in your place could have reacted in a variety of ways, all of them perfectly normal given the human nature. He could have wallowed in self-pity, dragging both himself and his friend down and making him feel guilty for his exclusion. He could have asked his friend to wait until they could run together. He could have resented his friend's achievement and would have tried to sabotage him. However, any of these approaches can sour relationships forever. While working out together as friends, jealousy, envy and other unpleasant emotions do affect your relationships, but remember, as best friends, you are a team every day. The best way out is to change your mindset and consider his success as your success. Help him prepare for the marathon. Accompany him to the event and cheer him up along the way. Remember, the key to happy friendship is not stand in each other's way, but to stand with each other, helping if we can, watching if we can't.

Vastu Tips

In order to overlook this setback, build confidence in yourself. You will be amazed to know how far one can go with a positive frame of mind. Lots of people who are successful say that the key to success is self-confidence. Simply by believing that you can achieve something, you can! Vastu Shastra suggests ways to boost your self-confidence. Meditate for half an hour every day and take time out for introspection and self motivation.

Another thing you need to ensure is to keep a positive approach. You have to have faith in yourself to achieve your goal. For this, Vastu suggests placing a piece of rock crystal on your table and to always carry a flawless piece in your pocket. This will not only magnify good energies to help you overcome the odds but will also keep envy at bay.

Friendless and Lonely

> I have no friends. Although, I do have a group of people I hang around with yet they are not really my friends. I have been trying to make a real friend since 8th class in my school and now I'm in 10th, but I have had no success. When I see all others having fun with their friends, I feel quite lonely and depressed. Can Vastu help me in finding a true friend?

Friends, especially good ones, are hard to come by. Lots of people feel lonely and don't fit in even when they have lots of friends and acquaintances. One of the best options is to take the initiative yourself to approach the person from the group, who you feel shares your interests and you feel happy in his/her presence. If you two click, it can result in a long drawn friendship, which you both will savour for years to come. To attract a potential friend, it is important that you extend a friendly hand yourself, even if you are the shy type, rather than waiting for him to do so. A lot of people misunderstand someone's shyness for snobbery. As a start, invite your fellow students to go to the movies with you. Or ask them to help you with an assignment, or offer your help to them, if they are having trouble. Or ask your teacher if you can work in groups for some of the assignments. This way you will get to know people and are sure to find a true friend.

Vastu Tips

Cultivating friends entirely depends upon the nature of an individual. Vastu Shastra suggests ways to develop a friendly nature that appeals to all and helps attract the right kind of friends. For this, first and foremost, you have to assess the location of your room as per the principles of Vastu. The most ideal locations are north, east, north-east or north-west of the house. It may also be located in the south-east but should never be in south or south-west. The correct location will help you develop the right kind of personality. If the location of the room is correct, take a look at the position of the bed with the room. You need to orientate yourself correctly enjoy the full benefits of Vastu. So, align the bed along the east-west axis with head towards the east since it inspires, enlightens and influences human nature.Take these steps and start winning friends in no time!

Ungrateful Friend

> My best friend asked me for money to pay her rent. Since she had brought me to the city, I felt indebted and gave it to her. But instead of returning it, she didn't even give me a call for over a month. Finally, she shamelessly called me again, asking for more money. I was flabbergasted! This time I refused point blank and she banged the phone on me. And

this is not the first time that it has happened. I am quite annoyed with her but don't want to break my friendship. How can Vastu help me in such a situation?

It is an unhealthy situation for you to be in. Your friend has taken you for granted and you seem to respond to her call readily. Though it is true that she has done you a good turn by bringing you to the city, it doesn't mean that you have to tow her line. Since you have never protested till now, she thinks you can be taken for a ride and is taking advantage of you. It seems that you still lack confidence and need other people's approval. This is perhaps driving you to help others all the time. You also didn't know how to say no till recently. So, people have been taking advantage of you. It is good that you have realized how you are being used and have got the courage to refuse a blatantly unfair request. You also realize that your friend didn't call you for a month after you loaned her the rent money and that the next call was for more money. By this it is quite evident where you stand in this friendship hierarchy in relation to her. All such people are best described as fair-weather friends who are out to fleece you. It is best not to count them among your friends.

Look for new friends with whom you can reconnect Such friendships will be on more even terms and they would also expect less from you. Train yourself to say no if anything is not acceptable to you. This way you will command their respect.

Vastu Tips

As per Vastu Shastra, your problem is of holding on to your money. You seem to be losing it in the form of giving loans to your friends. Have a look at your residence where you are staying. Is the toilet next to the main entrance? If it is then it is not a good omen because toilets represent waste and contain negative energies. It is also a container of still water that gets flushed down the drain. This is, metaphorically speaking, what happens to your money. You should make sure the door is always shut and that you place a mirror on it to deflect negative energies.

Another reason for losing money may be leaking taps in the kitchen or toilet Never ignore this problem because it literally signifies a leakage of money down the drain. Check all water leaks and get them rectified immediately.

My Best Friend Is all Over My Boyfriend

> My best friend has a major crush on my boyfriend and she had the cheek to admit it to me before I started going out with him. The problem is she keeps track of us, never lets us to be alone and openly flirts with my boyfriend. This not only irritates me, but also irks my boyfriend. How can Vastu cure her of this obsession?

If she is your best friend, then obviously her friendship means a lot to you. Why did you get into a relationship with a boy she likes? This is an open invitation to a major tension between the two of you that may even end a friendship. But if you really like this guy, you should have a talk with your friend and explain to her that even if she does have a crush on him, he is your boyfriend, and that you really can't stand it when she flirts with him.

If she has the tendency to invite herself to your outings, make sure you don't let out your plans until after they happen. If she gets upset that you are avoiding her, tell her that you like to be with him alone sometimes. However, assure her that you two can be together as before. Do things with her separately, but never make her feel that you are choosing your boyfriend over her because it can really hurt her feelings.

Vastu Tips

If there is anything in your bedroom that is in threes like candle stands or lights, curtains, chairs, pictures you could be attracting the presence of a third person. This physical manifestation of a real situation can be improved by adding or removing one item, so that the trio is turned into a pair.

Dominating Friends

> Even though I have a small circle of friends, they seem to be stepping over me all the time. I always go out of my way to help them, but they just don't acknowledge it. I don't expect too much out of them, but at least they should treat me as their equal and

not as a doormat. Is there a Vastu remedy to change their attitude?

Wherever you go in life, you will always find two kinds of people – those who like you and those who don't, no matter how hard you try to please them. So, don't waste your time on the latter kind. You have already displayed your courage by staying true to yourself instead of selling out your values to enter the 'in' crowd. You are obviously not fitting into your present crowd. If you abide by your values and decide not to be friends with snobs who treat you wrong, then you will find others who may feel the same way. So, connect with them and seek friends out of these like-minded people. Don't get discouraged if you don't find friends right away, just give it time.

Vastu Tips

According to Vastu Shastra, negative energies undermine self-esteem making one vulnerable to others. It is generally the waste or litter that gives rise to negative energies. There are certain things that you can ensure in your house. Never locate the toilet, which is a repository for waste, in the north-east corner, since it releases negative energies in the sacred area of the house. This adversely affects interpersonal relations. So, try and keep negative energies contained inside by always ensuring that the door to the toilet always remains closed and the toilet seat is always kept down firmly. Furthermore, to enhance the aura, place a few plants in the room and light a lamp or a candle.

Returning Gifts

> What, according to Vastu, is the best way to tell a friend that the gift she gave is not really usable without spoiling my relationship with her?

Many a times, it happens that we receive presents gifts of which we have no use. One way of tackling the situation is to ignore it and call her up on the telephone and appreciate her for this very useful gift and, later, as and when the occasion arises, dump it on somebody else. However, it is not a very honest way to deal with the situation! If she is really a good friend of yours then you can't afford to play games with her as you would yourself not like it. The best way out is to ring her up and thank her for her thoughtfulness in giving a gift and politely tell her that you don't use this brand of say nail polish or that colour of top or whatever you find wrong with the gift. Tell her that you know she won't be offended if she returns this gift to her since she is your good friend. Also tell her that she is giving it back to enable her to give it to someone else who can make really good use of it. This way you will not only return the useless gift to the rightful person in the most gracious and diplomatic manner but would also not offend your friend. In the end, your friend will appreciate you for your forthright approach.

Vastu Tips

For the above to transpire, there is a need to strengthen your friendship. Vastu recommends certain measures that bring you close to your friend. For a stable and a long relationship, there is a need to bring in as much positive energy in the house as possible. Since your friend, when visiting you, will occupy the social areas of your house like living and dining rooms, place red or yellow lights or lantern in the south-west corner of these rooms. Red and yellow lamps help bring positive sunshine energy into the house. Keep symbols of sun in these rooms as decorations. Look for paintings, which have scenes of the rising sun and similar themes. Make this change and see your bonds with your friend strengthening.

Paying Condolences

> A friend recently lost her longtime companion very suddenly in a car accident. What is the most appropriate way for me to condole, according to Vastu Shastra?

Most of us find it difficult to find appropriate expressions of condolence, especially in direct conversation. If you are in another town, send a card expressing your sympathy, saying how you heard the news and are thinking of her at a time, which must be very difficult for her. Some consider cards more effective than even attending cremation or prayer meetings, since there, one is just one of the crowds, just standing there with folded hands or hugging those one especially knows. However, this is entirely a personal decision. One point in favour of a card or a condolence letter is that it is not as fleeting as a personal visit at the funeral, since it is read at greater leisure. While writing, use appropriate expressions like 'May you have the strength to bear the loss' or 'I am thinking of you at this time'. Choose the words with sentimental thoughts that express deep sincerity to make it a really meaningful and well-written condolence note.

If in the same town, make a phone call, saying she must be going through an awful phase and feeling alone, and that your thoughts are with her. Offer to come and spend time with her, or perhaps meet for coffee. When you meet, say something like 'I was saddened to hear the news of his passing', and ask how she is coping. If the bereavement is of a sibling or a parent, use expressions such as 'I know at this time memories of childhood come flooding back...

Remember it is best to be sensitive and do something rather than leave the person alone. Most times during a tragedy it is best to be with people who really care even if at first, the instinct may be to mourn alone.

Vastu Tips

Death always saddens. You can do more than just condole the death of the favourite of your dear friend. Vastu recommends certain measures that can be suggested to your friend to ease her pain of the loss.

Your friend should keep all the personal effects of her companion safely and in a place where they can be accorded due respect. This, according to Vastu, will bring solace to the deceased and ease your friend's mind. However, these personal objects will be kept only till you decide to get on with your life.

❑

Chapter Seven

Relationship with Neighbours

"Excuse me Mr. Anand, your Chunnu has broken our glass globe on the gate," complained Bhalla staying next door to Anands. "I am sure it can't be my son. He is not the type to go breaking people's property," assured Anand. "But my wife has seen him doing it with her own eyes, Mr. Anand. Why would she lie about it?" countered Bhalla. "Bhalla ji, don't you know ladies, they always exaggerate things," retorted Anand. "What? Hold on! Don't you dare say anything against my wife or I'll sort you out," threatened Bhalla. "Do what you want Bhalla ji, just don't waste my time," said Anand raising his voice. And within minutes these next door neighbours were shouting down each other, forgetting the issue at hand, making a spectacle of themselves in the neighbourhood.

It is rightly said, 'you can choose your home but God chooses your neighbours'. Certainly there's no specific category of relationship that a neighbour fits into. The only thing you share with him is the proximity of living quarters. And here too, the dictum'good fences make good neighbours' rings true. If the people and across you can't stand the sight of you and vice-versa, the forced proximity certainly makes for very unwelcome living conditions. Hatred affects everybody health.

Good or bad, neighbours are neighbours and there is little you or anyone else can do about them. However, they are probably the only reason why living in a city can be most annoying and most reassuring experience ever. Remember the time when you were sitting alone in your quiet living room, getting thoroughly bored and desperately waiting for your family to return. When, all of a sudden, the doorbell rang and there on your doorstep stood your neighbour asking you to join her for a cup of tea, pulling you out of your depression. And God forbid, if you ever happen to trip down the stairway in the absence of your family, nine times out of ten, it will be your neighbours who will come to your aid. And this, irrespective of your equation with them! So, the next time you are raving about your neighbour, remember they may very well be angels in disguise!

Vastu Shastra stresses the importance of good neighbourly relations. You need to strengthen your bonds with those living in your proximity to maintain healthy relationships. There are a lot of people who continue to write to me for deliverance from their problematic neighbours. I have discussed a few problems in this chapter and recommended some Vastu solutions. They are guaranteed to help you in bonding with your neighbours.

Noise Nuisance

> I have recently shifted into an apartment with my family. Though it is nice and spacious, located in an up market neighbourhood, there is still a problem. The family adjoining us seems inconsiderate and makes a lot of noise that disturbs us. My wife has hinted about this to them a couple of times, but it seems they are not taking the hint. Can Vastu suggest some way to tackle this problem?

When you are stuck with a noisy neighbour, it is certainly no laughing matter. Noise can intrude into every area of your life and can literally assault you with its jarring effects. Whether it is boom boom of the heavy stereo music, lively parties, shrill alarms, loud conversations, hammering, revving, or some other form, excessive noise can affect the quality of your life, making you jumpy, irritable and stressful. Even houses and homes that have good insulation are often affected by modern sound making equipment such as amplifiers, DVDs, surround-sound systems and the like. The biggest nuisance is the night time noise since it echoes, carries more and can keep you awake the whole night.

In case you are being subjected to this form of punishment, it is best to take up the matter with your neighbours directly. Be courteous and polite, even if you are angry. For all you know, they may not even be aware of it! In most cases, once made aware, they will cease immediately. However, never approach the issue with the neighbours in the midst of a party as they may be drinking or partying heavily and may not want to talk to you. They may misinterpret your complaint as being against their enjoyment. So, approach them when you know they are home, when it's quiet and always plan beforehand what you are going to say.

There is a possibility that your neighbours may just not listen or are simply not interested in what you have to say and may persist in their noise making. They may deliberately raise the volume just to harass you further. In such a case, the best course is to inform them in writing. Though writing a letter to your next-door neighbours sounds formal, it gives you an opportunity to logically list out your complaints without losing cool or getting into an argument. Letters also serve good proof that you have brought the matter to the attention of your neighbours.

Vastu Tips

The problem here is that of interpersonal relationships between neighbours. According to Vastu Shastra, if the construction of the building in which one resides is flawed, then there is every likelihood that two people living side by side may not see eye to eye. For this, Vastu Shastra recommends certain remedies. Ensure that the main door of your house does not open directly opposite the main door of your neighbour's house as there is a possibility of negative energies entering into the house. Also ensure that there is nothing obstructing your main gate like boulder, pillar, tree, corner of another house, well, water sluice, streetlight pole, or waste bin, etc. A clear path will clear the lines of communication between you and your neighbour.

Parking Problem

> I am living in a colony where my immediate neighbour has bought two cars. The problem is that he has space for only one car inside his premises and the other car he parks in front of my house. This causes great inconvenience to me. I have tried broaching the subject with him a number of times, but he doesn't seem to understand. Can Vastu help me in driving some sense into him?

Every home seems to have more than one car these days, especially in up market colonies. Though the number of cars increases, the parking space remains the same. The result? Intrusion into each other's space.

The problem is compounded even more if there is off road parking.

Parking outside someone's house can cause a great deal of distress, which you may not immediately become aware of. Though one is not legally restrained from parking in front of someone else's house, neighbours often respect each other's unwritten or even unspoken agreements to respect parking areas. If we could all park outside our own homes it would be great but it's not always possible. Visitors and new people to the street may not realize that you like to park outside your home.

The best solution to this nagging problem is not to overreact. The neighbour parking the vehicle does not realize that this bothers you. Rather than shouting, have a friendly word and point out to him that you prefer parking right outside your house for security reasons. Tell him that if he insists on parking his car in front of your house, you will be forced to park in front of someone else's space that they require. You can help by giving him parking options. Many conflicts can be avoided through simple courtesy and communication. If your neighbours are decent, they will move their car and ensure that they don't park there again. If they are adamant on your space, inform them in writing. If this also doesn't deter them then maybe a quiet word with the local police officer may do the trick. Remember, at your end, drive and park, as you would expect others to drive and park.

Vastu Tips

Vastu Shastra recommends parking space away from the main building, preferably in the south-east or north-west of the house. South-east or *Agni* corner is ideal for locating the vehicle since it produces heat. The north-west west, the quadrant of air and movement, is also ideal because the vehicle is always on the move. If the parking space defending falls within these zones, retain space you are defending falls within these zones retain by all means. If they don't, then you may consider shifting from your parking space.

Barking Blues

> I have kept an Alsatian dog that just loves to bark. No amount of persuasion, threats or rewards deters him from this favourite pastime of his. It is not only proving to be highly disturbing to me but also to the neighbourhood and I have started receiving complaints. Can Vastu help me pacify my dog?

Though dogs communicate by grunting, whining, yelping, screaming, howling, growling, tooth snapping and panting, what they excel in is barking. Although barking is useful and normal as a means of communication, in excess, it can be a nuisance for the people who live in the dog's vicinity, especially the neighbours. Many people find it one of the most difficult problems to treat.

Barking to deter people from entering your property is fine, but if your dog barks continuously, it can become an annoyance. Unfortunately, your attempt to silence it by shouting is interpreted by the dog as barking and it continues undeterred and even redoubles its effort! One of the simplest ways to teach your dog not to bark is to teach it to bark on command. This way you will be able to introduce not only the command word for barking into its vocabulary but also to keep quiet!

Reward is, of course, the best motivation for good behaviour, so it's important to praise your dog when it's doing the right thing, not afterwards. This means rewarding it when it stops barking, and also when it doesn't bark in a situation, which would normally set it off. When your dog is lying quietly and allowing you to chat with visitors uninterrupted or when your neighbours come home and your dog doesn't bark, you can praise and reward it. This will encourage it to remain quiet the next time too.

Vastu Tips

To cure your dog of the menace of barking, you have to bring it down from its highly excited state to a less excited state. For this, it is important to locate your dog inside or outside the house according to Vastu Shastra. The place where you plan to keep your pet should never be attached to the eastern or northern walls. It is best to locate it in the north-west corner, away from the northern wall. This will pacify him and reduce his barking, letting you and your neighbours sleep peacefully!

Scourge of Smoke

I had purchased a bungalow to pursue gardening as a hobby, but my next-door neighbours are most inconsiderate. They burn dead leaves and other garden refuse near the wall adjoining mine both in the morning and evening. This causes suffocation and the stench hangs in the air for hours. My repeated complaints seem to fall on deaf ears and this is making me miserable. Is there a Vastu cure to persuade my neighbour to discontinue this annoying practice?

To stop this nuisance, you should take two steps simultaneously approach your neighbour and start recording this event that should include dates, times and the nuisance it caused. When speaking to your neighbour, see if you can reach a compromise. If you feel you can't talk to your neighbour, you should write to them. In most cases, your neighbours will listen to your complaint and amicably find a solution to the problem. However, if they don't then you should contact the local municipal department and lodge an official complaint. The officials of the department will take action to remove this nuisance forever. However, keep your written record intact in case your neighbours go to court, in which case you may be required to give evidence.

Vastu Tips

In this situation, there is a need for you to mend your personal relations with your immediate neighbours.

As you do so, you will find them warming up to you and completely ceasing this nuisance of smoke. Vastu Shastra recommends a few remedies for this. As a first step, ensure that your bungalow is enclosed within a compound wall from all four sides. This helps retain positive energies entering the premises and prevents them from escaping. These positive energies help give positive outlook to the occupants. Another important step is to ensure that the north-east portion of the compound wall is lighter and lower than the south-west. Even if you need to carry out renovation, make the wall in the north and east, thinner and lower and that in the west and south, thicker and higher. The difference in the height of the two walls should be one foot. Provide gates only at specified places. This will certainly help you mend your fences with your neighbour.

Two-timing Husband

> I have a close group of neighbourhood ladies and we gossip a lot. I recently came to know that one of the ladies of our circle is sleeping with another's husband! Though I have not let out this secret to the wife of that two-timing husband, the situation has become quite disturbing for me. How can Vastu help my friend deal with this situation?

Instead of getting disturbed about this piece of information, which may be nothing but hearsay, you should try to get to the bottom things and dig up some evidence. There are women who, because of sheer boredom, sensationalize stories that may be as mundane as a lady talking to somebody's husband. Assuming you are absolutely certain of what's going on, without a shadow of doubt, and you feel morally bound to do something about it, talk to the mistress, not the wife. Tell her that if the relationship with her lover is serious, she had better tell him to let his wife know someone else does. Possibly, the scare will put an end to the infidelity, in which case, let it drop, forget it, and never mention a word of it to anyone or allow it to become idle gossip. On the other hand, If the husband does tell his wife about what has been going on and she comes to you for comfort, do not add to her misery by telling her that you, or anyone else, knew about was going on. This way you will be there for her when she really needs you.

Vastu Tips

There is a need for you to extend a helping hand to the lady being betrayed by her husband, of course, without letting her know why. You should apply Vastu principles to her home so that good feelings are nurtured and grown within an environment that is conducive to ever increasing happiness between her and her husband. Make her guard against infidelity by ensuring that nothing in the home is set in the wrong place. Often, small corrections can avoid the many problems associated with infidelity. Does this lady have an aquarium at home? If she does, make certain it is not on the right-hand side of the main door, looking from inside towards the outside, irrespective of its compass location. This applies to all water bodies, whether inside or outside. Make these changes in her home and the erring husband is sure to return into the warm embrace of his wife.

Looking for a Husband

> A single lady of around 40 is staying in our neighbourhood. She is a successful professional and seemed to me to be leading an exciting life. During our conversation, I realized that though she seems happy yet in reality, she is increasingly growing bitter, as she hasn't found her Mr Right yet. Though I pointed out her good fortune in being a successful professional, she was not too delighted about it. I want to help her find a good husband. Can Vastu suggest some ways to get Mr Right for her?

It is good to be concerned about your neighbour and make her feel a part of your life. But that might not necessarily ease her concerns about her future life. Of course it is important that she values her profession achievements and appreciates the freedom you want to highlight to her. But acknowledge her anxieties too. Though you may try to put her at ease, never promise or even say that you are looking around for a perfect husband for her. This may make her repose unnecessary trust in you that you may not be able to fulfill, straining your relations. The trick is to try and make as much time as you can to do things with her. Talk of things other than home and family to subtly let her know that there is a life outside marriage. But at the same time keep looking for a good match for her and keep introducing her to new people. You never know when the cupid's arrow will strike!

Vastu Tips

In Hindu mythology, Krishna represents the eternal lover, charming the ladies with his melodious flute. This is probably why Vastu Shastra places importance of flute that signifies a state of perfect union between two people. So, present your neighbour with a flute or a painting depicting Krishna playing the flute and see her fall to the charms of her Mr Right!

❑

Part III
Relationships at Workplace

PART THREE

Relationships at Workplace

> *When one ceases from conflict, whether because he has won because he has lost, or because he cares no more for the game, the virtue passes out of him."*
>
> **–Charles Horton Cooley**

No relationship is without fighting and arguing and we all experience conflict both in our homes and workplace. At home, the mindset of the members is one of compromise, whereas at the workplace, it may not be so. There, more often than not, you have to contend with autocratic bosses, treacherous colleagues and unwilling subordinates, all out to ruin your career. Thus, interpersonal conflicts at the workplace can be dangerous and lethal for anyone. Some people call it personality conflict, where you can't seem to get along with a few people and often can't really figure out why?

There has always been a lot of interest in how to manage conflict once it appears in the open. But little thought has been given to preventing unnecessary conflict, so that it doesn't start in the first place. Most of us don't consciously manage conflict situations. It is normal to get caught up emotionally and just jump in without thinking. The core of conflict management involves slowing down and using your head to think though what you should do, rather than reacting in a Knee-jerk fashion. However, what distinguishes relationships that work from those that don't is how the arguing is done to resolve the issue. You can learn to fight fairly and actually reduce future arguments and the negative effects of disagreement. Many of us have not had a chance to learn fighting fairly due to lack of adaptability and immaturity. If you can learn to change the words you use, you will succeed in reducing unnecessary conflict at the workplace.

Most of the time, the problem of workplace conflict is one of communication, both yours and how the other person communicates. If you have met people who seem to get along with everyone, you might have wondered what it is that they do to create such great relationships. It is likely that they are actually communicating quite differently from people who seem to create conflict wherever they go. If you change your communication ability, you can significantly reduce conflict around you.

We all have to deal with difficult people at some point in our lives. Some are lucky enough to encounter difficult people only on rare occasions, while some may deal with them everyday of their working lives. Whether you deal with difficult co-workers or hostile customers, frequently or rarely, one of the best defenses against them is to know yourself well enough to be confident about your 'difficult people tolerance threshold'. You must learn how to deal with difficult people and diffuse hostile situations.

To resolve conflicts, as also to tackle difficult people at workplace, you need to bond with your bosses, superiors, colleagues and subordinates. Vastu Shastra suggests remedies at workplace to bring about positive changes in your relationships with your co-workers. Adhering to the principles of Vastu at workplace not only enable you to achieve harmony but will also make you grow richer in love and friendship. Let us take a look at the various relationships at the workplace and what Vastu Shastra recommends for improving them.

❑

Chapter Eight

Relationship with Boss

Krishna entered the office with a little trepidation. He had not been in the best of terms with his boss for the past couple of days. And today he was late. He half expected his boss to welcome him with biting sarcasm, as was his typical style. As he stepped into the office, he saw his boss standing at the reception and speaking on the telephone. He braced himself for a barrage of explanatory calls but, to his surprise, nothing of the sort happened. His boss glanced at him and continued to attend to his call, ignoring him completely.

Krishna went to his seat and waited to be summoned by the boss, but the call never came. He was not even called for briefings, though he held the important post of graphic designer in this advertising agency. Instead, his boss pitted a junior graphic designer, Mohan, against him by calling him for the job briefings. Krishna felt humiliated but tolerated this outrage and even outwardly displayed that he doesn't care, but inside he was seething with rage like a simmering volcano ready to erupt. It was only a matter of time when he did.

"*Since when have you started taking briefing on my behalf, Mohan,*" asked Krishna sarcastically. "*Hey relua Krishna! Because you were late for the office, boss called "me for the briefing,*" clarified Mohan. "*And now that I have come?*" goaded Krishna. Before Mohan could open his mouth, the boss called him into his office for instructions, leaving Krishna out once again. This was the last straw for Krishna and he rushed to confront his boss hurling accusations and shouting at the top of his voice. That was the last day for Krishna in that agency.

Welcome to the hard reality of the workplace. If you are already or are about to become a victim of your boss, Vastu Shastra can come to your aid. I have produced certain live situations with suggested Vastu remedies, which will certainly help you resolve your workplace conflicts with your boss to a large extent.

Leave Spoils Relations

> I am working as a marketing executive in a private firm. I always had a great working relationship with my boss. All was going fine until I took a few days leave to attend to family problems and that too after convincing my boss about it. However, after rejoining, I feel he is giving me a cold shoulder and leaving me out of important meetings. How can Vastu help me in winning back his confidence?

Without good communication, a difficult situation could become intolerable, when a little clearing of air would take care of it. Remember, you never want to actually confront your boss but you can always discuss things with him. First ask yourself, were you able to state your requirement of leave clearly enough or was there a communication gap. There is a possibility that you may not have specified your 'few days' and your boss may have been expecting you earlier.

Did you leave your boss in lurch regarding the workload, when you proceeded on leave? If you did, because of pressing home problems, did you ensure their completion immediately on rejoining? There is possibility that you may not have even remembered them!

Your best course of action in such a situation is to catch your boss in a good mood and ask outright if there are any other problems. Do not confront but do it very tactfully. Since you had been a good employee and always had great working relationship with him, let him know how much you enjoy working for the company and for him. Keep the lines of communication open and work hard to win a place in his heart once again.

Vastu Tips

According to Vastu Shastra, the layout of office greatly influences interpersonal relationships, especially between the boss and the employees. An incorrectly laid out office may lead to spoiled relationships and discontentment amongst staff. If possible, place your chair towards the south or west wall so that you face the auspicious north, east or north-east while sitting. This would infuse you with positive energy, helping you impart a positive frame of mind to your boss, thus projecting you in a favourable light.

Aspiring for Promotion

> A vice-presidential position has recently been vacated at my company and I, along with a few of my colleagues, am eligible for it. Every one of us is eyeing that position. Can Vastu help me in convincing my superiors that I am the perfect fit for the position?

To become a contender for this position, it is evidenth that you have been networking with your superiors in the company, putting your best into each project you handle and showing them what a great asset you are company. If you are really vice-president material the second step is easy. Find out who is in the selection committee and what skills are of main concern to him. Prepare your marketing portfolio and reflect those top five or six skills with proven examples of how effective you are in those areas. Use examples from the things you have already accomplished for the company. Reflect those proven skills in additional dollars earned for the company or in increased clientele. Send it to the decision maker along with a letter of intent on your finest paper and keep networking!

Vastu Tips

You need Vastu to help create most amicable relationships in the higher echelons that can assist you in successful networking. To activate relationship and enhance the possibility of your selection for the coveted position, find an office with a door facing north-west. If you cannot find such a door, then adjust the furniture in your office that enables you to sit facing north-west. This would help you to pull your seniors towards you and make you the centre of attraction.

Raise Not Realized

> I am facing a peculiar problem. After persuading my boss for days, I managed to get a raise and was very happy about it, but just after a month he reverted to my same salary, saying the raise was unjustified. This has made me quite angry and I am thinking of quitting, though I like my job. Can Vastu help me restore my raise?

Your first step should be to approach your boss tactfully, and ask him how you don't justify the raise. Show him, once again, what an asset you are for the company and in what ways you have profited the company. There is a strong possibility that certain vested interests are envious of your raise and are provoking your boss against you. It is your duty to show your boss the truth and get him out of the quagmire of treachery. If your boss is still adamant and fails to respond satisfactorily, the decision to quit or continue in the same pay scale rests with you. But before you arrive at a decision, evaluate if your boss could legitimately afford what he first promised. If you also honestly feel that he can't afford the raise, be gracious. In case you do decide to quit, don't lose heart, there may be bigger, better opportunities waiting for you elsewhere.

Vastu Tips

As any Vastu expert may tell you, you need to take Vastu steps to rein in your money that presently is showing a tendency to vanish. For this, you need to evaluate your house. If the level of floor of your house is higher in the north than in the south then there is a problem. This means that wealth, which enters from the north, the direction of wealth, doesn't remain, but is being drained out towards the south. The solution is to raise the level of at the southern part. If this is not possible, light a lamp in this corner.

Another problem may be the location of the water tank. If it is located in the centre of the house then there is a problem. This signifies a definite stagnation of wealth since water must always be in motion. There is no alternative but to remove this tank and replace it with a fountain, if you so desire.

Late Hours at Work

> I am a working woman with small children. Lately I have been instructed to work late by my new boss and it is placing a great strain on my husband and children. Previously, I

used to leave my office at around six in the evening, but now I have to stay till eight. I am scared to express my concerns about this extended time to this boss as he may think that I am disloyal to the company and my job. Can Vastu help me solve my problem?

You state that your boss is new. There is a possibility that your boss, who has recently acquired this new position, is working hard to accomplish his goals to prove himself. Give him your full support and help him succeed in his new role. In building this bond of trust, you and your family may have to cope up with the inconvenience of late hours for a few days till you gain enough confidence to discuss your personal matters with him.

At an appropriate moment, when your boss is relatively free and in a happy frame of mind, broach the subject that is troubling you. Express your problems politely and in a professional manner, stating how it is affecting your job and the company. At the same time, apprise your new boss about your contributions to the company and your continued efforts towards achieving his goals. This kind of approach will surely make your boss see the point. However, at your end, be sure to make your work hours highly productive so that the results speak for themselves. Offer to take work home from time-to-time that you can complete after your children go to bed. For this, you will need to plan your work schedule at home so that you are able to manage it without sacrificing quality family time.

Vastu Tips

You can strengthen your relations with your new boss by getting rid of all the negative energies that are afflicting you at your workplace. Find out the direction of your table. If it is directly in front of the door, it means that all negative energies are focussed straight at you. And you become the first to be attacked! You should move away from the door. Vastu recommends removing your table from the path of the door and turning it to face east or north. Facing these directions of wealth and wisdom, while working, will infuse you with positive energies giving you the power to compel your new boss to sympathize with you.

Job Stress

> I am handling a big project for my company and am working a lot of late nights. I have started to feel worn out and irritable at work. It seems that my boss is not acknowledging my hard work and my co-workers are secretly making fun of me for working so hard. This is making me mad. I am afraid I may flip my lid and spoil my relationships with everyone in the office permanently. Can Vastu show me the right path?

You sound burned out and probably physically exhausted too. Your symptoms are indicative prolonged stress that is taking the form of harbouring false notions about your co-workers. My suggestion is to catch up on your sleep by taking a day off. Be out of touch. Turn off all, your phones, leave the laptop at work and tell everybody you will be incommunicado, irrespective of what happens. You may have to overcome considerable resistance from within and from others, but if you want to heal yourself, go through with it. Having a breakdown at work will only harm you. On the other hand, you will be much more productive if you take rest and get refreshed.

During your day off, read, walk, listen to music, get a massage, anything that helps you relax and forget your work. Then take some more sleep. Sleep helps your Body repair itself, improves cognitive processes and generally makes you feel better. Once you are well rested, examine whether your job is really meaningful to you and how? You might reduce its demands on you. Learn to take a break, especially at night! Take care of your physical and emotional needs too by staying connected with friends, getting exercise and eating right.

Vastu Tips

Vastu Shastra has many suggestions to bring tranquility into your life. It seems that there is something amiss either in your home or office that is making you stressful. One of the major causes of stress and irritability is clutter. It can invade a home as well as the workplace. If you have too much clutter and piling up of unused things all around, it is bound to obstruct the free flow of energy, thus accumulating negative energies. You should clear out the junk you don't need and stack the rest in an orderly manner.

If you have red curtains in your bedroom, replace them with light green ones. Red keeps the mind restless and adds to stress, whereas green calms it. For tranquility, have tall trees and plants in the south-west and small plants in the north-east. The tall shrubbery helps in blocking the negative energies of the setting sun, whereas small plants allow positive energies of the morning sun, bestowing serenity.

If possible, face north or east while doing your project in the office. This will leave your mind undisturbed and enable you to focus better on the job at hand. Make it a point never to sleep with your head towards the north. Since it is the north of the body, it repels the magnetic north agitating the mind and disturbing your sleep.

Totally Tied-up with the Job

> Since the time my husband's boss has diversified into a different brand segment, my husband has started spending more and more time in this new venture and is left with no time for the family. This is making us quite unhappy and we miss the family togetherness we used to have. When I point this out to him, he says that his boss is solely depending upon him for the success of this new venture. I feel that my husband

is being used. How can Vastu help me in enlightening my husband that he is being taken for a ride?

You have brought up a problem that is widespread in our society, namely work holism. Bosses are cunningly adept at identifying workhorses, like your husband, a keep them piled up with work. If your husband is one such scapegoat, then you may have a problem on your hands. Simply pulling your husband away from work is not going to solve your problems and may create some for him at his workplace. However, if your husband is simply trying to avoid the family in the name of work then you have another kind of problem. Workaholics will have us believe that if they don't spend so much time at their jobs, this world might come to an end. However, work holism is a problem that can have many reasons like drinking, depression, anxiety, marital unhappiness, affairs and so on. So, your first step in solving this problem is to identify the problem. Ask yourself whether you have had any marital trouble with your husband even before he began working such long hours?

In case your husband's boss is exploiting him, you need to discuss and plan with your husband how he can restrict himself to the laid down office hours without hassling the boss. Encourage him to talk to the boss to convince him on this issue. However, in case your husband is keeping late hours due to marital disharmony, you need to talk straight with him before the issue gets out of hand. If he is keen on improving his relations with you, this discussion will help him know your feelings and may bring him back into your fold and revive your family togetherness.

Vastu Tips

There is a possibility that your husband feels that his professional expectations are not being met. This can be extremely discouraging and may have made him a workaholic. To help him achieve his expectations, Vastu Shastra recommends that you keep a piece of rock crystal on his table or make him carry a flawless piece in his pocket. This will magnify good energies and make him achieve his expectations.

In case you feel that your husband is avoiding the family, rejuvenate love by shifting the bedroom from north-west to south-west. The north-west corner makes one restless, whereas a southwest corner stabilizes life and enhances feelings of love.

Keeping an indoor plant in the north corner of your house or the drawing room would help in sorting out the problems up to a great extent. Also keep a red rose in your bedroom in the south-west corner in some crystal bass to enhance the love energies.

Affair with Boss

My best friend, who is also my flatmate, is sleeping with her married boss. She insists they are in love and he has promised to leave his wife, but I think he is lying. Since she is living with me, I feel responsible for her and am afraid that if she distances herself from the boss he may fire her. Can Vastu help me in convincing her that the affair is wrong?

It is difficult to talk someone out of love. You are only free to tell your friend that you don't approve of her affair. Doing so may make you feel better, but probably won't make any difference to her because, in all probability, she is doing this favour for retaining her job. Whatever may be the case, she must learn to accept responsibility for her own decisions, actions and mistakes. However, the best thing you can do for her is to approach her boss's wife indirectly and let on about this affair to her. This will surely put the breaks on the affair and will help the boss make up his mind about leaving his wife. At the same time, encourage your friend to expand her circle of friends. She might find a suitable single man to hook on to!

Vastu Tips

The problem here is to wean away your friend from her boss without her losing her job. This, according to Vastu, requires certain actions that can diminish negative energies, which seem to be surrounding your friend. Since she is your flat mate, find out which directions does she keep her head while sleeping. If she keeps it in the north, then there is every likelihood that she is under stress and facing negative influences. Take steps to remedy this by suggesting that she sleeps with her head towards south or east. These directions will infuse her with positive energies and help her see the correct path. Also find out which direction she faces while working in the office. If she is facing south, then she is inviting negativity. Persuade her to adjust her desk to face east or north. This will grant her wisdom to get out of the mess she has put herself into.

❑

Chapter Nine

Relationship between Superiors and Subordinates

"Sir, my daughter is very sick, I want a few days leave," pleaded Ram Niwas with his foreman. He was a factory worker for the past ten years and had never got promoted. The foreman was new to the factory and could not say no to such an old worker and said, "Look Ram Niwas, we are already short of manpower and we have to meet an important deadline. However, since you are one of the oldest workers, I will grant you your leave. How many days do you require?" "At least three days as my daughter has to be shown in the city hospital," replied Ram Niwas. "You can go, but make sure you rejoin duty on time," said the foreman. "I promise, I will return on time," assured Ram Niwas.

Ram Niwas proceeded on leave and the foreman adjusted his duty hours amongst the other workers, as was the norm. "Sir, he will not come back before a week," said one of Ram's co-workers, "it's his habit. But the foreman was adamant. "No. He will surely, return as he has given me his word." Three days passed and the foreman expected Ram Niwas to rejoin duty on the fourth day. He did not turn up. Four days stretched to five and then to a whole week. Exactly the eighth day, he rejoined duty.

"This is how you repay me for my kindness?" yelled the foreman the moment Ram Niwas enter factory."Sir, you don't know what I have been through.

I did not get any conveyance to go to the city for the first two days. Then I had to wait for two more days for doctor's appointment," explained Ram Niwas. "Don't tell me stories, Ram Niwas. Everyone in the factory knows your habit of overstaying leave. And that is probably why you have never been promoted," scolded the foreman. This really put off Ram Niwas who shouted, "I don't care what everyone knows and I don't care for you or my promotion. You can do what you feel like. I will report this matter to the Union and they will bring you to your knees," challenged Ram Niwas. "And I will report you to the manager," countered the foreman.

And there goes another relationship down the drain. This everyday occurrence is a stark reality in today's workplace, where relationship between superiors and subordinates holds the key to the smooth functioning of a company. If this incident sounds familiar to you, then you may be a victim of your superior or at the receiving end of your worker. Vastu Shastra can come to your aid in such situations. A few live examples that I have encountered during my practice and their Vastu remedies will certainly help you resolve your workplace conflicts.

Problem Solving

> I work in a factory that manufactures spare automobile parts. Since I am new to the job, I keep facing one problem or the other at the workplace. However, when I approach my superior for guidance, he seems to ignore me and if I persist, berates me in front of others. This is affecting my job performance and peace of mind. Can Vastu cure this problem?

When someone doesn't have the answer or doesn't want to answer, they are tempted to ignore the problem. If this has been happening to others too, then it is quite obvious that your boss is professionally incompetent and doesn't know his job. In such a case, your superior may escape by ignoring the problem, but it is not the solution. He can ignore problems only so long, until they grow far larger and far harder to resolve. In such a situation, you can consult your colleagues and find out a collective solution to the problem that may range from discussing the matter with the superior to reporting against him.

Another possibility is that he doesn't want to spoonfeed you by giving you ready solutions. He may be trying to make you self-reliant in your job. In case this is what your superior is aiming at, make a conscious effort to find the solutions to your problems yourself. In case you feel simply bogged down by them, make an effort to explain this to your superior. He may be reluctant initially and may even discourage you, but once he sees your sincere approach towards your work, he will change and go the extra mile in helping you out.

Whatever be the case, you would do well to tell him not to berate you in front of others. This will put a caution on him and force him to curb his habit.

Vastu Tips

The problem here seems not so much about work about interpersonal relationships between a super and a subordinate. Vastu Shastra suggests ways to mend these relationships. If you are staying in quarters provided by the company, opt for one that is in the south-east or north-west and never take the one in the south-west. The right directions will infuse you with positive energies and optimism to handle your work situation to your advantage while bringing cordiality in your relations with your co-workers and superiors. While at workplace, carry out your assigned tasks facing north or east. This will always keep you in a frame of mind and help you to work out your problems.

Ignored at Work

> I am in the customer servicing department for a finance company. It is our superior's responsibility to delegate us our clients for servicing. For quite sometime, I have been noticing that my superior assigns all

the prestigious clients to other executives leaving ordinary ones for me. Though it does not have any bearing on my performance, I don't like this discrimination. Is there a Vastu way to stop this injustice?

It is evident that your superior is assigning duties based on the abilities of those under him. It needs a bit of introspection on your part to see if you are professionally as competent as your colleagues. If you think you are, it may be that your superior is unintentionally assigning you unglamorous clients. Many a times, he remains unaware of this inadvertent discrimination till it is pointed out to him. To him, as long as the project is being successfully completed, it doesn't matter who does a better job or is more committed.

If your superior is deliberately delegating less prestigious clients to you, then it is a cause for concern. You can tackle this situation by tactfully pointing out the alleged discrimination. But never confront him about this, since it will only antagonize him and in no way help solve your problem. While discussing, remember to stick to the specifics of your case and never generalize or he may get offended. Give proof where you felt discriminated and listen carefully to his justification. In most cases this exercise will resolve the problem. In case, your superior is guilty of high handedness, this discussion will impose caution on him. However, if you feel that your superior is not adequately redressing your grouse, don't hesitate to take up the matter with other seniors up the ladder.

Vastu Tips

Whether your boss is intentionally keeping you out or you don't seem competent enough to him, the point is that you fail to catch his eye. To make yourself conspicuous, it is important that you take certain Vastu steps. First inspect your office; find out whether the door is opening to a dead wall? If it is, then you are experiencing major communication problems that will ultimately lead you to a dead end. Ideally, the best way to remedy this fault is to open the dead wall by installing a window on it. If this is not possible, hang a mirror on it. It will enhance positive energies and reflect your personality and help make you popular with your co-workers.

Promotion Dilemma

> I am a manager in a company and am facing a dilemma. One vacancy for supervisor has been created in my department and I have two equally qualified persons for this position. One claims that the position should go to him because has earned it by turning in three solid years. But the other has been the top producer for the

company. How can Vastu help me decide would be a better supervisor?

Promoting one of your people and not the other is a tough decision to make. There are several things to look for besides longevity with your organization. However this line of thinking can become tricky because a person with seniority feels that he automatically fits the bill just on the basis of his experience with the company. 'You should consider three main criteria before you arrive at a decision.

The first is reliability and loyalty. Can this person be counted upon? Do you expect him to continue to contribute to the growth of your company? The second is their actual accomplishments. Has this employee done something to make a profit for the company and will he continue to do so? Finally, is this person pleasant and tactful with his co-workers and will he be able to handle the disgruntled employee, who has not been promoted? If an individual meets these criteria, don't hesitate to give him the promotion.

Vastu Tips

The problem that you face in such a situation is of the right choice. This will have a bearing on your reputation as a senior. You need Vastu to enlighten you and infuse you with wisdom to help you make the right decision. Correct location of your workplace will help you in this task. The most suitable direction for locating your workstation is the north, north-east or east of the office. These directions bestow farsightedness, enhance Wisdom and improve the powers of judgement. East is particularly good, since it is the direction of inspiration and enlightenment. However, locating the study room in the north-west, which belongs to the realm of air and movement, is likely to make you restless, unfocussed and indecisive.

Problem Perfectionist

> The manager under whom we work is too much of a perfectionist. He drives us crazy trying to make sure everything is always done correctly at the workplace. This is putting too much stress on us. Can Vastu help in calming our boss so that we have an easy time?

If your boss is driving himself crazy, then he is really too much of a perfectionist! Perfectionism is generally driven by anxiety and by a deep feeling that one is not good enough in whatever one does. These anxieties may result from the demands of the family made on him as a child or may have been contributed by an emotionally abusive person who was bent upon proving him worthless. It may also be his escape from emotional pain.

Your best course should be to find out what scares your boss. Is it the fear of rejection or humiliation, if things are not perfect? Is it the worry of underperformance and someone finding out about it. Once you get an inkling of what exactly is bothering your boss, win his trust by doing his bidding to sometime and then persuade him to go easy on himself. Such kind of people always remain stressed. Take help of his family and friends to impress upon him the virtues of stress management, daily workouts, massage, meditation and other outlets, and encourage him to take life as it comes.

Vastu Tips

According to Vastu Shastra, one of the major causes of any kind of fear of fear is the type of entrance to a house. If it is dark and gloomy, it is bound to create bad feeling. Causing fear and apprehension. If your boss has this kind of an entrance to his house, it will certainly influence him in his workplace and may take on varied forms, like perfectionism. To prevent this, you can advise him to enhance energies entering his house by making the entrance bright and welcoming. Make sure he has enough artificial lighting at the entrance, if there is no ingress for natural light. He can also liven it up with plants or flowers. These help absorb the negative energies.

Promotion Blues

> I have recently been promoted to a new position, but I have been told by my senior to continue doing many of my old duties. This has left me overwhelmed. Many of the tasks cannot be delegated to staff. I wake up at night wondering how I will get through

> the work, but don't want to tell my senior in case she feels I am not up to the job. How can Vastu help me cope up with this workload?

Promotion always comes with more workload and responsibilities. The thing that is upsetting you is your belief about what is possible and what might happen. This is causing you excess stress and worry. Honestly evaluate whether you are really up to the new job. Truthfully answering it now would save you from stress and the stigma of poor performance. If, on the other hand, you feel capable of undertaking your new job along with the workload of the old one simultaneously you should not hesitate to discuss it frankly with your senior. Instead of asking her, think through the problem and demand what all you would need to get the work done without jeopardizing the quality of work. Tell her what work would need to be re-assigned and what additional resources may be required for it. This professional approach to the problem will persuade your senior to give a serious thought to your points and resolve your problems to a large extent.

You at your end should also change your thinking from what can't be done to what can be done and how it can be accomplished. When you evaluate your tasks, determine those, which must be done by you, those that can be delegated or re-assigned to someone else, and those that really don't need to be done at all any longer. Prioritize and organize all your responsibilities, since not everything has that same relevance and urgency.

Vastu Tips

It seems that basically you are a negative thinker and need to infuse positive ness in your life. Vastu suggests ways to do it. Observe your worktable; if the light fixture behind you casts a shadow on it then you will be imbued with negative thoughts. Your solution is quite obvious, either adjust the angle at which you sit or change the light fixture on the wall or, better still, use a table lamp.

Another factor that may contribute to your pessimistic outlook is a dingy and gloomy workplace. Working in dim light or in a place where natural light has no access, is not only unhealthy but induces negativity. For this, ensure that doors and windows are kept open for natural light. In case this doesn't solve your problem, then keep a light burning during the day. Positive influences will help convert your pessimism into optimism.

Turning Down Promotion

> I am in senior management at a fortune 500 company and have just been offered a promotion. However, I have two young children and the new position would require considerably more travel and I am not sure whether I will be able to spend that much time away from my family. However, if I

turn down the promotion, it may ruin my chances for promotion later. How can Vastu help me decide the best course?

Turning down a promotion is a bit risky. Unfortunately, there is no guarantee that opportunities will be available again in the future. However, it is important that you follow your heart. Having a position that requires considerably more travel and more responsibilities will undoubtedly pull you away from your family a lot more. Your children will only be young once!

You must first decide your limitations and communicate them straightforwardly. The best course for you would be to sit down with your superior and have a very honest discussion and let him know when you felt ready to pursue advancement opportunities. If you want to be re-considered for future opportunities, be sure to state that you will consider advancement and more responsibilities in the future. Tell him that your concern is to do exceptional work for the company and you will be unable to do this if you remain overly concerned about leaving your family so frequently. In the meantime, continue to perform at exceptional levels at work and get recognized for your outstanding accomplishments. Stay abreast of other opportunities as they develop. Once you become more comfortable with balancing work and family, speak with your superior again and let him know that you are ready to be considered for advancement. If you are a strong candidate for promotion and have proven yourself, I believe other opportunities will come along. However, getting promoted to the wrong position can be even more detrimental to your career than not accepting a promotion. If there is a choice, opt for a position with less travel for which you should be willing to wait. Keep developing the skills that will lead to growth opportunities either for your current employer or for another company. Develop a career plan that's in sync with your family and personal commitments. Focusing on your priorities and making conscious decisions will help you enjoy your life!

Vastu Tips

To have things your way, you should do things in your house the Vastu way. First and foremost, remember that exposed beams influences our well being, and may have an effect on our job. Its effect primarily depends on the ceiling height, the type of beams—structural or weight bearing, time spent under the beam and the physical and mental strength of the person under the beam. A large structural beam can make you highly susceptible to stress that will negate your chances of working towards your promotion. So, in order to keep yourself in a charged state and look after two kids, you would require either removing the beam or if that is not possible, taking steps not to sleep or sit under it any time. Only after this action, will you be able to excel in your job and be in contention for promotion.

Make sure your bed room is also clutter free and the east corner is not burdened in any way.

Habitual Latecomer

> I just can't seem to shake off the habit of always arriving late to the office every morning. Though I am late only by six to 10 minutes, but I am late. My supervisor has warned me from time to time that cures me of this ailment only for a couple of days, but again I restart. I want to stop this before it becomes an issue. Can Vastu help me in my quest?

Being late all the time is not very serious. Truly troubled people turn up hours late or not at all. It may be that like a movie star you want to be noticed by making a grand entrance. May be you are afraid that nobody will pay attention to you otherwise, which may mean insecurity is at the root of your chronic tardiness, or you may, like many procrastinators, simply lack discipline. Simply exercise a little will-power and common sense. Set clocks and watches 10 minutes fast. Carry a kitchen timer around the house; let the alarm tell you when to get out of the shower, finish dressing up and leave the house. This way you will establish a routine that will see you at the office bright and early. However, exceptions are always there, you may always indulge in some 'latecoming' sometimes if your mood so dictates!

Vastu Tips

If you are in the right mood for a thing, you will certainly carry it out, in time, every time. Vastu has suggestions to enhance your mood to make you reach your destination on time. If the walls or surroundings are done up in dark colours, the negative energies associated with dark colours have to be dispelled. It isn't enough to brighten up a dark room with artificial and natural lighting. You have to complete the process by using light coloured wallpaper. This will brighten up your environment and help you to view everything positively, even reaching office on time!

❑

Chapter Ten

Relationship with Colleagues

"Well gentlemen, I would like to place on record the excellent work done by Raman in preparing this report. It is not only meticulously executed but also has been well researched. This is the kind of work that I expect from all of you, and not the one I highlighted in our last meeting," stated the Chief Editor, while Atul squirmed in his chair. It was his report that was cut to pieces by the boss in the last meeting. "I will just circulate this report to you, see for yourself why I have marked it as outstanding," continued the boss. As the report reached Atul, he gave it a quick glance and found nothing out of the ordinary in it. It was a run-of-the-mill kind of report and Atul could bet anyone anything that his report was better than this. As he looked at Raman, sitting self-importantly with a triumphant smile lighting up his oily face, he could not help but feel outraged at the boss who was blatantly siding with Raman, trying to promote him while undermining his own standing in the publication.

"Shikha, did you find anything outstanding in Raman's report?" asked Atul after the meeting. "No. But if the boss says it is good, it is good," replied

Shikha tactfully. Atul felt small, he was expecting Shikha to blow the report to pieces. Had she done so, he could have started an office gossip against Raman, but she sidestepped the issue neatly leaving him fuming alone. From that time on, Atul resolved to get even with Raman, by hook or crook, and regain his lost honour.

Do you feel envious, if your colleague does a fantastic job on a report? If you do then welcome aboard to competition bandwagon! More than 55 percent executives surveyed recently said competition among co-workers is more prevalent now than it was 10 years ago. Friendly competition can be healthy and can help boost productivity, but seniors should avoid creating an atmosphere in which employees feel pressured to outperform at the expense of others and the company. Workplace rivalries interfere with results because the desire to get even generally gets in the way of achieving goals. Thus, it is important to create an atmosphere of collaboration by promoting trust and a common purpose amongst colleagues and co-workers.

Vastu Shastra can help create such a helpful atmosphere merely by rectifying the structure and correctly placing the components within your workplace and home. Try the Vastu remedies given herein that have been tried and tested in a number of situations arising from workplace rivalry.

Passed over for Promotion

> I am working in a retail chain outlet as floor manager. Though I am hardworking and result oriented, my colleague, who is better qualified, has recently been promoted and has become my senior. Seeing him enjoying his success is getting me down. Can Vastu help me in coping with this setback?

Ever so often it happens in our career that despite putting in our bit, we are overlooked for promotion. However, remember that money, titles, promotion are all great but they are no guarantee for happiness. After all, it is happiness that every one seeks in life. Learn never to stake your happiness on this single aspect of your life. In career, like everything else in life, you sometimes win but sometimes you lose too. If you let others treat you on the basis of your professional performance, you will wind up throwing away your personal life. If your emotions depend upon your career, you are going to be a nervous wreck. Ups and downs in life continue; you should get up and try again in every way not only in your career but in every other aspect of your life. You have to keep moving on. If you are set to change yourself, you will surely make a positive change in your life. It is best to enjoy the present, whether good or bad, because there is no going into the past and no guarantee of the future.

Vastu Tips

It is natural for the mind to get agitated and getting passed over for promotion is certainly a serious setback. What you require is to calm your mind by infusing tranquility into your workplace. Vastu Shastra suggests some remedies that will help you overcome this disappointment. Have a look at your workplace and see the placement of your desk and computer. If their placement is incorrect, it can affect your thinking and behaviour. Ideally when you face the computer monitor, you should be looking towards the north-east. This direction of wisdom and wealth bestows positive energies and banishes disruptive and depressing thoughts. Even if you don't own a computer, always sit facing the north-east.

Quarreling Colleague

> I am a marketing executive in a big firm and doing well in my field. However, I have a problem. My colleague always remains at loggerheads with me in whatever I recommend. He always disagrees with me and tries to shoot down my proposals. We indulge in lot of arguments and this makes me miserable. How can Vastu help me bring about cordiality between us?

Everyone argues. Disagreements are an inevitable part of people trying to co-exist. While every relationship has disagreements, the number and severity of those disagreements vary tremendously.

You are never going to agree on everything and you shouldn't even try. But one vital agreement will help you reduce the pain of disagreements—choosing a method for your discussions. It is not uncommon to find two people in a relationship with widely differing ideas about how to deal with conflict. Some rush into it the first moment they notice the problem, others hint around the problem without directly stating it, and still others try to avoid the subject and perhaps the instigating event altogether. You can win all the arguments you want and feel good about always being right, but you would not have helped yourself in the slightest.

The real problem arises when you two adopt different approaches. This forces you to deal with the conflict at hand and the difference gives rise to tension. You must realise that resolving conflict is an important step to your advancement. Level the playing field in your discussions by deciding how you can air concerns to each other without arguing. Remember, it is not your colleague against you but you and your colleague against in the problem. Try and build a climate of cooperation instead of competition, so that peace can be restored between you two. If you start working practically at solving this problem, it can be nipped in the bud. And ways follow what Mahatma Gandhi preached, "Don't bring your opponents to their knees, bring them to their senses".

Vastu Tips

Wherever there are two co-workers, rivalry is bound to occur. However, Vastu Shastra suggests ways in which you can arrange your workplace to minimize competition and introduce an atmosphere of Cordiality. Mirrors are known to cause rifts. They always create extremely powerful changes in the flow of energies. When they are placed in correct orientation, they bring a great deal of happiness, but when they are set in wrong places, they fracture interpersonal relationships. If you have a mirror in the workplace, ensure that it does not reflect your table, as it causes differences with co-workers. If it reflects the door to your office, all the positive energies present in the office will be lost and you will never be able to accumulate. So, the best way to prevent the mirrors from affecting you is to keep them covered at your workplace. This way you will be able to infuse tranquility and mend your spoiled relations.

Low Self Esteem

> An overbearing colleague at the workplace keeps questioning my competence through veiled insinuations. Though I am well qualified for my position, this continuous insinuation has cast doubts in my mind about my own worth. How can Vastu help me restore my self-esteem?

Your colleague is totally unjustified in doing this and you should not take it lying down. However, before you do anything about your colleague, ask yourself why do you take his insinuations seriously? Are these feelings of inferiority a result of some incident in your childhood? A maladjusted child can internalise deeply negative beliefs about himself even when his peers or parents did not mean to convey that at all.

You can help restore your self-esteem by creating deeply meaningful affirmations like how competent and successful you really are and repeating them regularly during the day. This will boost your confidence and you will be able to face your tormentor at the workplace without getting affected.

Vastu Tips

Even the most competent people fail to advance in their careers because of low self-esteem. Vastu Shastra can help in the restoration of your professional dignity. One of the best methods to overcome lack of self-confidence is meditation. It is amazing how you can transform yourself simply by half an hour of daily meditation. Simply by believing that you can do something about your problem, you can!

In order to rejuvenate your mind to face your overbearing colleague, ensure that you are not sitting under a beam or a low ceiling. Sitting underneath will always keep you under pressure making you susceptible to your colleague's jibes. Since this is a structural problem and may not be easy to resolve, you can try and mitigate the damage by fixing magnets on the ceiling or a mirror to widen the distance metaphorically. The magnets reorient electromagnetic waves, which get distorted by the iron content in the beams.

Detested Colleague

> I have discovered that I can't stand a co-worker because, instead of getting the job done, she is essentially making excuses for her employees. She complains about how they are overworked, whereas everyday they all leave the office by 6 pm and take a two-hour lunch break. Confronting her on this issue was highly upsetting for both of us, as she accused me of being a heartless male. Though, I have decided not to broach this subject with her anymore, she continues to irritate me by her behaviour. Can Vastu suggest ways to channel my irritation and effectively communicate with her?

What you describe is a fairly common work issue, that is, dealing with difficult colleagues. The first thing to remember about such interactions is that you yourself tend to create an issue out of a non-issue! It may be that her personality or the way she makes excuses reminds you of a family member you have problems with or even of some aspect of yourself that you don't like. Take some time to think about this possibility.

Also, sit down with a co-worker you trust and write down all the things that bother you about your other colleague. With your co-worker's feedback, refine your reactions into one or two basic themes. For instance, does your irritation with her boil down to the fact that you think she is irresponsible, that she doesn't pull her share of the load, that she gets special treatment from management?

Once you have figured out this theme, think about how you can convey your points to her without losing your temper. Try to convey your thoughts without getting into a parental or authoritarian stance. For instance, you could say, "I hear you saying that your employees are all overworked, but I have noticed that most days they take long lunches and are always out of the office by six. It just doesn't make sense to me, can you explain your point of view?" If she responds defensively—"You are really exaggerating, they only did that once in the last month," then you could counter with "Well, I observed that happening on April 1, 5, 6, 7, and 8 of this month. Was there something unusual about that period of time?" and so on. You need to think out what you want to convey and use facts and examples, rather than blaming or general criticism. Once you hear her side of the story, you will be less hostile towards her.

Vastu Tips

Hostility against colleagues at workplace is a grave problem and has to be solved if you want to continue in the company. Vastu Shastra suggests remedies for curing irritability that results in hostility. Examine your office, if the entrance is towards the west, it means that you are letting in disruptive energies. This, being the direction of the setting sun, makes us contemplative and we tend to think our opinions are right. To curb your argumentative nature and produce more harmony, put a copper wire on the doorframe to neutralise the negative effects.

If the walls of your office are covered with irrelevant charts, maps or graphs, Vastu Shastra considered it as clutter and the same gets reflected in your emotions and attitudes. If there are too many things reminding you of your hatred colleague at your workplace in the office, you can be sure that this co-worker will not eye-to-eye with you, as you are sub-consciously influenced by these images. Remove all clutter from your office.

Guilty Feelings

> The company I work for laid off about ten per cent of the staff last month. Several of my friends lost their jobs. Every time I speak to them I feel guilty that I was retained and they weren't. How can Vastu help me to get over this feeling?

You are in a difficult situation, especially since the layoffs are so recent. It is best to tell your friends about your guilt and ask them if they are harboring any negative feelings towards you. If they are, this will give them a chance to level with you. And you should not inordinately fear this direct question because in all probability, the worst you will hear is that one of them is somewhat envious of you, that he realises the feeling is irrational and will not let it affect his relationship with you.

To get over your guilt feelings, try to help them out by offering job leads and other assistance. Your mere asking and giving a sympathetic ear to their feelings would give them a huge support. Never take personally, if somebody should direct his frustration at you or does something negative to you. Try not to react to their negativity and wish them well, even if you find that you need to distance yourself for a while.

Keep reminding yourself that the layoffs of your friends were out of your hands and that it is not your fault. Think that these layoffs are an opportunity to take a new and satisfying career path. A door closing also means a door opening. You can be concerned and responsive to your friends' situations, without taking" responsibility for them.

Vastu Tips

There is a grave necessity for you to overcome your guil as it can affect your job. Vastu Shastra suggests some ways, which can help you in getting back in the right frame of mind. All kinds of emotions including guilt are a result of negative energies produced by some fault in your home or workplace. If they lack cleanliness and have garbage dumped in the open, then it may make you susceptible to negative energies, that magnify your emotions creating ill health and discords. So, keep the litter well under cover and don't let even brooms lie out in the open.

Pointed objects, like hanging electricity cables, broken glass, etc., outside the main door of your home or inside your office, give off negative energies. To promote harmony and suppress your guilt feelings, ensure that these things are either covered or screened from view. Once you rectify these defects in your home and workplace, you will find yourself cured of your guilt feelings.

Competition Blues

> I am quite frustrated. Whatever I do at my job, my colleague seems to do it better. Recently, we both were given the same kinds of projects with a deadline. I worked day and night at it and submitted it quite well in time. My colleague submitted it two days late. Even then my boss rated his project better than mine without even taking note of the fact that he defaulted on the time schedule of submission. How can Vastu help me get even with him?

Rivalry at work is a common phenomenon and everyone experiences it one time or the other. However, if this competition becomes unhealthy, consuming you with so much hatred that you seek revenge then it is time to sit up and take note. First of all, make it clear in your mind that the boss is looking at the quality of the project and not on the time schedule. If by spending two extra days your partner can turn in better work, your boss will certainly prefer him. The need of the hour is to sharpen your skills, gain expertise and give your colleague a run for his money. You need to come into the eyes of your boss through your work and not through your rivalry!

Vastu Tips

Vastu is used for making your surroundings, whether at home or at workplace, so conducive that you prosper in all spheres. Whenever, this kind of thing happens, there is every likelihood that there is some fault in the house or in the office either structurally or in the setting inside. If there are stairs going down into your house, it means that you are literally moving downwards instead of upwards, towards darkness instead of light. What you need to do is try and level out the entrance and remove the step or steps. If this is impossible, try and mitigate the effect by keeping plants on the steps.

Jai Mata Di.

❑